WHAT TO DO
WHEN YOU DON'T
KNOW WHAT TO DO

WHAT TO DO WHEN YOU DON'T KNOW WHAT TO DO

A Christian Teen's Guide to Coping

RANDY SIMMONS

GOSPEL ADVOCATE COMPANY
NASHVILLE, TENNESSEE

Unless otherwise indicated, scripture quotations are from the Holy Bible: New International Version, © 1973, 1978, 1984, International Bible Society. Used by permission of Zondervan Bible Publishers.

Published by Gospel Advocate Co.
1006 Elm Hill Pike, Nashville, TN 37210
http://www.gospeladvocate.com

ISBN: 0-89225-423-8

TABLE OF CONTENTS

I DON'T KNOW WHAT TO DO!

What do you do when you don't know what to do? What do you do when you don't see any good way out of a bad situation? What do you do when you don't see any direction? What do you do when you've done everything you know to do about a problem and you still don't see much hope for progress?

Mandy was 16 years old. Her parents were not Christians; in fact, they discouraged her from being involved with the church. Nevertheless, Mandy had become a Christian at age 13 and really loved the Lord. She was very active in the church, participating in all the youth group activities.

One summer day Mandy came to my office, and through her tears she said, "I need to talk to you real bad. I have made a mistake, and I just don't know what to do." Mandy had a first-time, one-time sexual experience with a young man and, as a result, she was pregnant. When she told her parents, they said, "Young lady, you will either have an abortion quickly, or you will be out of this house!"

Feeling the enormous pressure from her parents, Mandy violated her conscience and her spiritual beliefs, and had the abortion. Now she was tormented by that decision and the consequences of it. Her words of inner agony still ring in my ears:

"Every time I hear a baby cry, I just about go crazy. I don't know what to do anymore ... I just don't know what to do."

Joe was in his late teens. His parents were Christians but were not very dedicated to the church. Joe was a "good, old boy." Deep in his heart he wasn't a bad person, but he placed a great emphasis on having "fun," and he didn't want anyone to tell him what to do. He just wanted to do his own thing.

Joe started his quest for fun by drinking, and then slowly moved to illegal drugs. After a while, the temptation to pick up some extra money to fund his growing drug habit got the best of him. Late one spring night, Joe was arrested and charged with intent to distribute cocaine, which is a felony. On one occasion, as I was counseling him before his court date, Joe said, "I just don't know what to do."

So many young people today are mirrors of Mandy and Joe. All kinds of problems or experiences may enter our lives that cause us to cry out, "I don't know what to do." This book is designed to help you learn what to do when you don't know what to do.

COMMON TRAPS

First, let's consider some common traps that many young people today fall into when they don't know what to do.

Some teens turn to alcohol. They attempt to cover up their inability to make tough decisions by avoiding them or drowning them. Of course, this only creates more problems, as "in the end it bites like a snake and poisons like a viper" (Proverbs 23:32).

Others turn to drugs when they don't know what to do. In ever-increasing numbers, people are choosing artificial highs and lows through illegal drugs. They need pills to get them started in the morning and pills to get them stopped at night. They need drugs to alter or change their thought processes instead of altering their thoughts according to the wisdom of Philippians 4:8: "Finally, brothers, whatever is true, whatever is noble, whatever is right, whatever is pure, whatever is lovely, whatever is admirable — if anything is excellent or praiseworthy — think about such things."

Still others turn to illicit sexual activity when they don't know what to do. The enormous problems of teenage pregnancies and the widespread outbreak of various sexually transmitted diseases such as herpes, syphilis and gonorrhea are evidence of people searching for answers and searching for fulfillment in body, rather than in spirit and soul. This obsession with sexual experimentation has helped create the most deadly disease in the history of mankind — AIDS. The statistics concerning AIDS are brutal: One out of one dies. Of course, the guilt and emotional harm that results from promiscuous sexual behavior is devastating enough even if one somehow escapes disease. These ills are a heavy price to pay for not knowing what to do.

Of particular concern is the increasing number of teenagers turning to suicide when they don't know what to do. Suicide is second only to accidents as the leading cause of death among teenagers. The *Ft. Myers News Press* ran the tragic story of 13-year-old Tonya DeHahn of my city. Tonya was not the typical suicide victim. She was bright, attractive and carried a "B" average in school. She didn't appear to have problems on the surface, and her parents and friends had not noticed any significant personality changes. On the night before she took her own life, she curled up in bed with her mother and father while they were watching television and had a few laughs with them. The next afternoon, when the DeHahns returned home from their jobs, they found Tonya's body in the bathroom. With methodic perfection, she had folded back the rug, lined up the shampoo bottles on the floor, crawled into the tub, pulled the shower curtain closed, and shot herself in the head with a .22-caliber pistol. She had carefully planned every detail. She left this note:

Dear Mom and Dad,

It's not your fault. You did not do any-thing wrong. I just don't like my life. All my stuff goes to y'all. I love my computer. Mom, don't have a heart attack, OK? Because I love y'all, and I don't want y'all to die be-cause of some reason like me. I hope God lets me come to heaven because I want to see Granny and Grandad, but that's not why I'm killing myself.

I guess I better go. Y'all are going to be home soon. I'm up in the bathtub because thought maybe the blood would not mess much up in there. I'll see you in a while if God will let me come visit you. Sorry that I didn't do my homework or chores, OK? I love y'all forever.

Tonya

Her suicide hit her family and friends like a ton of bricks. She had shown none of the usual early warning signs. From all practical appearances, she had it all. But she didn't, did she? She had reached a point where she didn't know what to do, and like some 30,000-40,000 teenagers each year, she turned to suicide when she didn't know what to do.

WHAT TO DO

What do you do when you don't know what to do? We all face problems and difficult situations where we temporarily don't know what to do. What do we do then?

I am so delighted to tell you that when you don't know what to do, you don't have to turn to alcohol, drugs, illicit sexual activity, suicide or anything else detrimental to you. When you don't know what to do, God has very carefully and clearly given you a formula for what to do. Here it is:

> Trust in the Lord with all your heart and lean not on your own understanding; in all your ways acknowledge him, and he will make your paths straight. Do not be wise in your own eyes; fear the Lord and shun evil. This will bring health to your body and nourishment to your bones (Proverbs 3:5-8).

This is what you do when you don't know what to do. You search for something that brings health and spiritual strength and nourishment. What is that something? Let's break Solomon's words down into smaller bites so that we might learn what to do when we don't know what to do.

1. Trust in the Lord with all your heart. Put the problem in hands bigger than your own, hands bigger than anyone else's on this earth. Don't commit the problem to yourself, or any human being — put it in the hands of Almighty God, the Creator, your heavenly Father. If this sounds like a simple answer or a cliche, it is because Satan loves to create doubt in your mind. It is not a cliche, it is reality. It is a great eternal truth inspired by the Holy Spirit of God. You must trust in the Lord with all your heart. That is a major part of the solution when you don't know what to do.

2. Lean not on your own understanding. Our own understanding is very limited. Self, at its very best, is still not very good (see Romans 7:15-25). The great apostle Paul had the same dilemma we often have. He didn't know what to do. He said, "I want to do good, but I end up doing wrong." And he said, "I'm a wretched man! What can be done for me? Who can rescue me?" In other words, "What do I do when I don't know what to do?"

What was his own answer to his own problem? "Thanks be to God — through Jesus Christ our Lord! So then, I, of myself, in my mind am a slave to God's law, but in the sinful nature a slave to the law of sin. Therefore, there is now no condemnation for those who are in Christ Jesus" (Romans 7:25-8:1). Paul came to the same conclusion that Solomon came to by the Spirit of God. That is, when you don't know what to do, don't trust yourself or your own understanding — trust the Lord!

3. In all your ways acknowledge Him, and He will make your paths straight. Did you catch that? In all your ways acknowledge Him. The simple truth is, many of us don't know what to do because we have mixed-up priorities. We want to live one life at church and another life out in the world. We want to use one kind of language at church and another kind of language out in the world. We are often like the person James described in James 1:8: "A double-minded man is unstable in all his ways" (KJV). So, Solomon wrote, "In all your ways acknowledge him." That means all your ways — your ways at home, at school, at work, on the ball field and in your recreation, as well as at church.

We cannot separate the acknowledgement of God to some small segment of our lives and then expect to know what to do when problems come and tough decisions must be made. Acknowledging Him in all your ways means all your ways. It means we have to so internalize these three truths that we make them a part of our lives. It means that all of our actions and all of our decisions are dependent upon trusting the Lord and leaning upon Him. That is what it means to acknowledge Him in all your ways.

Most everything we do in life depends upon the decisions we make. We are responsible for our own choices and decisions, and when we don't know what to do, we must return do God's Word and do what it says. Very simply, we are to:

- Trust in the Lord with all our hearts
- Lean not on our own understanding
- In all our ways, acknowledge Him

That, my friends, is what you do when you don't know what to do!

TALKING BACK

1. What do you do when you don't know what to do? How are you most likely to act when you don't know what to do?

2. Think back over some of the common responses to not knowing what to do mentioned in the lesson (alcohol or drug abuse, promiscuous sexual behavior, anxiety, etc.). Do these solutions work? Explain you answer.

3. In your own words, describe what it means to "trust in the Lord with all your heart."

4. Why is your own understanding inadequate for some of the difficult circumstances of life?

5. How do you "acknowledge" the Lord? Complete this sentence: When it comes to my relationship with God, I acknowledge Him by ...

EXERCISING YOUR FAITH

1. Memorize Proverbs 3: 5-6. It might save your life some day.

2. Write out a short essay on this subject: "What I Would Tell A Friend Who Was Stressed And Didn't Know What To Do." You may save a friend's life some day.

TEMPTATION

Jack was 17 years old, handsome, a popular student-athlete at school, and a leader in his church youth group. Having been raised in the church, Jack knew right from wrong, and he obeyed the Gospel at age 15. Jack loved the Lord and meant well, but as he sat across from me in the city park where we had met to talk, he repeated the words that all of us say at some time or another:

> I don't know what to do about the temptations I face. It seems the more I pray about my temptations, the more they haunt me. I try to surrender them to God, but the next day they are right back, and I fall back into sinful habits. What can I do about these stubborn temptations?

Jack's experience is certainly not unique. In fact, it is normal. It is wrong to believe that once we become Christians, we no longer struggle with temptation and sin. To the contrary, we can often expect temptations to intensify. After all, the more we mean to God, the more we mean to Satan because he is trying to destroy the work of God.

Being a Christian is a wonderful life. Our sins are forgiven. God is our heavenly Father. Jesus is our Lord and Savior. The Holy Spirit is our Counselor (John 14:15-27). Christian friends encourage us. And we are destined to experience victory forever in heaven. But our "sinful nature" (NIV) or "flesh" (KJV) is still with us and constantly battles the Spirit of God: "For the sinful nature desires what is contrary to the Spirit, and the Spirit what is contrary to the sinful nature. They are in conflict with each other, so that you do not do what you want" (Galatians 5:17).

As we study what to do about temptations, we will use the question method, focusing on four major questions about temptation:

1. What is temptation?
2. Why do we have temptations?
3. What is the pattern of temptation?
4. What can we do to overcome temptation?

First, what is temptation? Basically, temptation is that feeling or inner voice that says, "Go ahead and do it" when you know you shouldn't. Temptation is the work of Satan. Temptations always have a "tempter" behind them. Scripture calls Satan "the tempter" (Matthew 4:3; 1 Thessalonians 3:5). His primary work is to keep us away from God and lead us into sin by appealing to our "sinful nature."

Satan is very powerful, and temptation is very strong, but it is important to remember that he is a limited being. While he may trouble you and tempt you, Satan cannot control you, unless you allow it. Satan's power was broken by Christ's sacrificial death and victorious resurrection. First Corinthians 10:13 promises, "No temptation has seized you except what is common to man. And God is faithful; he will not let you be tempted beyond what you can bear. But when you are tempted. he will also provide a way out so that you can stand up under it."

Second, why do we have temptations? Jack asked me that day, "Why doesn't God just destroy the Devil, or at least why doesn't He decrease the strength of temptations?" Good question. None of us knows for sure exactly why God allows everything He does. However, Scripture offers us some reasons why God may allow temptations:

Temptation may be God's method for testing our love for Him. When Abraham was commanded by God to offer his only son, Isaac, as a sacrifice on the altar, he

16

must have been tempted to say "no" to God. How could God expect a man to kill his son? But Abraham made preparations to obey God. Just at the last minute, God stopped the sacrifice, revealing His real reason for testing Abraham: "Now I know that you fear God, because you have not withheld from me your son, your only son" (Genesis 22:12). We know that Abraham loved God because he obeyed Him when all the passions of his heart must have been crying out to disobey Him. So, God may allow us to prove our love and loyalty for Him by saying "no" to stubborn temptations.

Temptation may teach us important lessons. All Christians undergo hardship. James 1:2-4 teaches that trials help develop our character. If you see your temptation struggles only as a problem, you may never learn all that God wants to teach you through them. God can use our temptations to perfect our character and teach us spiritual lessons (1 Peter 4:12-13). As we learn to trust the Lord and resist temptation, we grow and mature as Christians. Always remember that when you say "no" to temptation, you are really saying "yes" to something far better — spiritual growth and maturity in Christ!

Temptation may reveal our weaknesses and emphasize His strengths. The apostle Paul was given "a thorn in my flesh, a messenger of Satan, to torment me" (2 Corinthians 12:7). Perhaps this "thorn" was a temptation he struggled to resist. Three times he asked God to remove it, but God refused, and His answer came back, "My grace is sufficient for you, for my power is made perfect in weakness" (v. 9). Paul then wrote, "For when I am weak, then I am strong" (v. 10). If you are bothered by a particularly difficult temptation, hang on to God's grace and power. Recognize that your weakness can be His strength.

Third, what is the pattern of temptation? A passage in James clearly reveals the pattern that temptation always follows: "But each one is tempted when, by his own evil desire, he is dragged away and enticed. Then, after desire has conceived, it gives birth to sin; and sin, when it is full-grown, gives birth to death" (James 1:14-15). Temptation always follows this process:

1. We are tempted by our own evil desires.
2. Instead of resisting the desire at this point, we are "enticed" and draw closer to the sin.
3. We yield to the temptation and sin.
4. Instead of repenting and turning from the sin, we continue in it, allowing it to grow and lead to spiritual death.

Probably, the best example of this temptation process is the first time it was used (Genesis 3:1-7). The Devil went to Eve in the appearance of a snake with the purpose of trying to get her to disobey God. Notice how the pattern developed with Eve:

1. Her desire grew when she "saw that the fruit of the tree was good for food and pleasing to the eye."
2. She listened to Satan's lies and drew closer to the temptation rather than resisting it and running from it.
3. She not only committed the sin, but encouraged Adam to do likewise.
4. Sin entered the world for the first time, leading to the possibility of spiritual death.

Now, how might this process of temptation play out in your life? Let's say you are tempted by your "own evil desire" — that may be drugs, sexual sin, jealousy or any sin. Let's imagine that it is drinking alcohol. Here is how the scene often plays out:

1. You like the feeling a few drinks gives you. It is enticing and appealing to you (that is temptation). Some friends come along and invite you to go out with them to a party where most people will be drinking alcohol.

2. You debate the temptation in your mind. You know it is wrong. God would not approve. Your parents would not approve. But what is the harm in just going along to the party? So, you go ... and draw closer to the sin.

3. At the party you first resist the offer of a drink, but people keep offering it to you and encouraging you to drink. Finally, you accept a drink ... then two, then three.

4. One party leads to another, and you become addicted to alcohol. Your spiritual life declines, and your sin either leads to physical death (alcoholism, drunk driving accident, etc.) or to spiritual death, or both.

Is there a way this story could have been changed for the better? Certainly! Consider this scenario:

1. You like the feeling a few drinks gives you. It is enticing and appealing to you (that is temptation). Some friends come along and invite you to go out with them to a party where most people will be drinking alcohol.

2. You debate the temptation in your mind. You know it is wrong. You pray about it. Hopefully, with God's help, you will decide not to go to the party at all because it would tempt you further. Maybe you don't know about the alcohol and decide to go to the party, but you commit to yourself and God that you will not give into any temptation of sin.

3. At the party you are offered a drink several times, but each time you ask God for strength to say "no," and you refuse the offers. You seek out others who are not drinking and encourage them. You leave as soon as you can and find a better place to visit with your friends.

4. You have avoided the temptation to drink either by not placing yourself in an environment where you will be greatly tempted to do so and relying on God to help you.

WHAT TO DO?

This discussion leads to our final question concerning temptation: *What can you do to overcome temptation?*

1. Realize that we will struggle with temptation as long as we live. All people must struggle with temptation. Even Jesus battled with Satan over temptation (Matthew 4:1-11). And Hebrews 4:15 says Jesus was "tempted in every way, just as we are — yet was without sin." We must recognize that our being tempted is not a sin; sin takes place only when we give in to temptation.

2. We should avoid circumstances, situations or people that put us under heavy pressure to sin. First Thessalonians 5:22 instructs us to "avoid every kind of evil" (NIV), or to "abstain from all appearance of evil" (KJV). This means that if certain people tempt us to sin, we might have to back off from them. It means we should be selective about the kinds of movies we see, the television programs we watch, and the magazines and books we read. We can defend ourselves against many temptations by simply avoiding tempting situations.

3. Accept responsibility for your sins when you have given in to temptation. Every time something goes wrong, we tend to blame someone or something else. We may blame our parents, our friends, God, Satan or a number of other people in an effort to avoid accepting personal responsibility for our sins. Avoid playing "the blame game," and simply confess your sins to the Lord and trust Him for forgiveness.

4. Use the Bible to help you hold off the Devil's attacks. That's what Jesus did in Matthew 4:1-11. He met every devilish temptation with a quotation from Scripture. After Jesus used the Word of God three times against Satan, "Then the devil left him." We can use the same tool Jesus used against Satan!

> I have hidden your word in my heart that I might not sin against you (Psalm 119:11).

> Resist the devil, and he will flee from you. Come near to God and he will come near to you (James 4:7-8).

5. Seek the support and encouragement of a Christian friend when faced with temptation. Seek out someone who will help you turn away from sin without turning away from you. It's easier to avoid temptation if you can find a friend who will pray with you and for you, and check with you at regular times to see how you are doing.

6. Realize that we have God's promise that He will never allow us to be tempted beyond our power to resist, and that He will "provide a way out." Look back for one moment at 1 Corinthians 10:13. God is faithful! He will provide a way of escape from temptation. But we cannot expect God to help us when, at the same time, we are preparing to disobey Him! Be sure that you "clothe yourselves with the Lord Jesus Christ, and do not think about how to gratify the desires of the sinful nature" (Romans 13:14). Don't overmatch yourself with Satan by flirting with temptation. Instead, cooperate with God by obeying Him, and He will give you victory over Satan and temptation!

By the way, Jack has made it so far. He is serving the Lord happily and, for the most part, is winning the battle over temptation. You can, too!

TALKING BACK

1. Have you felt the power of temptation? How would you describe it?

2. How would you answer the question, "Why doesn't God just destroy the devil, or at least why doesn't he decrease the strength of temptations?"

3. What is the typical pattern or process of temptation?

4. How does temptation differ from sin? Is it a sin to be tempted?

5. Six suggestions were given in the chapter for overcoming temptation. Which, if any, of these suggestions work for you in fighting temptation?

EXERCISING YOUR FAITH

1. Write out 1 Corinthians 10:13 and put is where you will see it every day (mirror, door, bed, etc.). Let the truth of this temptation fighting verse sink into your soul.

2. Complete these sentences:
   "My sins are forgiven because ... "

   "Because my sins are forgiven, I can ..."

STATEMENT OF INTEGRITY

In administering the test on heredity, I, as your teacher, placed a great deal of trust in you, the student. I had complete faith in your honesty and integrity. In grading the exam, however, I have found it quite obvious that several students have violated my trust and shown a lack of integrity. While this dishonesty cannot be overlooked or excused, I feel that it would be to the advantage of every student to make a statement of the way(s) in which he or she was less than honest and, in making this statement of truth, to help restore his or her integrity to some degree. I also want to provide an opportunity for those who were completely honest to reaffirm their integrity with a signed statement.

Check those statements below which apply to you, and then sign your name in the blank provided.

___ I looked at someone's answers.

___ I allowed someone to look at my answers.

___ I gave someone else answers verbally.

___ I received answers verbally from someone else.

___ I took a copy of the test from the room before the exam.

___ I had access to a test that was taken from the room before the exam.

___ I and someone else found one or more of the answers by working together.

___ All of the answers that I put on my paper were not entirely the result of my own study and research, and reflect the work of someone other than myself.

Signed _____

Each answer entered on the test paper that bears my name reflects my own study and thought, and that of no one else. The test score I receive will be wholly the result of my work alone.

Signed _____

GUILT

As a high school sophomore at David Lipscomb, I loved sports and girls and hated biology. My teacher was likable enough, but biology was just not my subject. When a group of fellow classmates worked out a plan for cheating on an important test, I shamefully joined in with them.

I passed the test but felt very guilty. I knew I had done wrong, not just because I might get caught, but because the act itself was wrong. Within a few days my troubles compounded when my biology teacher confronted the class with his suspicions that much cheating had taken place during the last test. He decided to give each of us a second chance at being truthful, by passing out the form on the opposite page.

I quickly and truthfully checked the fourth and eighth blanks and signed my name, thereby receiving an "F" on the test. But I learned greater lessons that day than any biology lesson could ever teach. First, cheating is not only wrong, but it doesn't pay in the long run. As Numbers 32:23 teaches "Be sure that your sin will find you out." Second, even if your sin does not find you out instantly, a troubled conscience can produce much guilt.

"I just feel so guilty" is one of the common statements heard by ministers and counselors. Feelings of guilt can haunt and plague a person, provoking negative emotional symptoms such as anxiety, depression, pessimism, fear, insomnia and the like.

Guilt is usually the result of a troubled conscience responding to sin. It can be a persistently negative emotion, worsening when one refuses to confess his or her sin and receive forgiveness. For instance, my guilt over cheating on that test nearly two decades ago likely would have taken one of two courses had it not been resolved at the time:

1. *The guilt would have continued to plague me indefinitely.* My feelings and emotions may have been played out in a number of negative ways, but the underlying problem would have been guilt. Unresolved guilt resulting from unconfessed sin can trouble a person for a long time.

2. *The guilt could have been suppressed to the point that my conscience was "seared" (1 Timothy 4:2) and I no longer felt any guilt, sorrow or regret.* The Bible teaches that it is possible to deaden the conscience through continual sin, until we are no longer sensitive to guilt.

Guilt is a stubborn emotion. It demands a decision from us. We must choose to confront the guilt and its causes and gain freedom from it — or we choose to avoid or deny the guilt, thereby allowing it to grow like a cancer within our souls.

How do we try to avoid our feelings of guilt?

A common way we attempt to deny guilt is by blaming others for our problems. In the Garden of Eden, Adam began the "blame game" by blaming Eve for his sin, and Eve attempted to pass the buck by blaming the serpent. So blaming others for our sins is as old as sin itself, but in the final analysis, it doesn't help us because in doing so we are still is avoiding the real problem — our own guilt.

Sometimes we attempt to evade our guilt by excusing, defending or rationalizing our actions. Much of today's "pop psychology" attempts to blame all of our actions on our environment, but that is largely a cop-out for accepting personal responsibility for one's behavior, attitudes or actions.

Often people try to relieve guilt by punishing themselves. They believe they must pay a heavy price for their sin, and guilt is the price on the ticket. They may even take this a step further by interpreting every unpleasant circumstance in their lives as God's way of punishing them. How much easier it would be to simply confess the sin and claim God's forgiveness and cleansing.

Other people may be driven by guilt to do good deeds, but for the wrong motives. Perhaps a parent takes his children out to a movie in the evening because he shouted at them that morning. It would be better not to shout in the first place! Even church work can be done out of guilt or improper motive (1 Corinthians 13:3). Good works may suppress guilt, or even help one deny it, but the guilt will soon surface in some form.

Many people seek to avoid unresolved guilt through the use or abuse of alcohol, drugs, food or anti-social behavior. They try to escape their guilty feelings by drowning them in alcohol, dulling them by drugs, or misusing food (overeating or undereating). This only compounds the problem of guilt by adding another problem of addiction.

I hope you can see that sins tend to multiply in the soil of guilt. The sin that so troubles you today most likely sank its roots into your life yesterday. And make no mistake about it — Satan is very skilled at using your past to ruin your future.

WHAT TO DO

Can you have a new beginning? Yes! The apostle Paul wrote, "Therefore, if anyone is in Christ, he is a new creation; the old has gone, the new has come!" (2 Corinthians 5:17).

What can you do about guilt? Let's discuss some important principles for handling guilt and finding freedom from its devastating effects:

1. *Identify the cause of your guilt feelings.* Frequently, this can be done very easily as was in the case of my biology test. At other times, however, the causes may not be as apparent. Whenever you feel the agony of guilt, begin by asking yourself honestly, "Why do I feel guilty?"

2. *Confess your sin to God in prayer.* First John 1:9 reads, "If we confess our sins, he is faithful and just and will forgive us our sins and purify us from all unrighteousness." We must first own up to our sins, and then we must disown them. As you confess your sins to God in prayer, do not worry about surprising or shocking Him. After all, you won't be letting God in on information He doesn't already know! So be honest and sincere in confessing your sins to God.

3. *Trust God to "forgive and purify", as Scripture teaches.* The Bible says that God is "faithful" "and "just," meaning that He is trustworthy and reliable. He will keep His word. What does God promise to do with our confessed sins?

> *"As far as the east is from the west, so far has he removed our transgressions from us" (Psalm 103:12).* Why do you think the psalmist says east and west, as opposed to north and south? Because there is a limit to northerly and southerly directions. Once one reaches the North Pole and goes beyond it, he is then traveling south again. But there is no limit to easterly or westerly direction; the psalmist, David, used that illustration to describe God's limitless forgiveness of our confessed sins.

> *"You will again have compassion on us; you will tread our sins underfoot and hurl all our iniquities into the depths of the sea" (Micah 7:19).* Consider how far God sends our confessed sins away. The deepest known point in any of earth's oceans is Marianna Trench, located in the Pacific Ocean. There the ocean is 36,198 feet deep, nearly seven miles from surface to ocean bottom. Micah used the depth of the sea as an illustration of how far God removes our confessed sins from us.

"Their sins and lawless acts I will remember no more" (Hebrews 10:17). This passage echoes Jeremiah 31:34. God is not only a good forgiver, He is a good forgetter! He no longer remembers our confessed sins. Satan remembers them and constantly brings our sins before us, creating guilt. The cure for such guilt is to continue confessing your sins and keep telling yourself, "God says I am forgiven and purified!"

"Therefore confess your sins to each other and pray for each other so that you may be healed. The prayer of a righteous man is powerful and effective" (James 5:16). Once again, God's Word promises that confession of sin brings healing — in this case, healing from guilt.

4. Fully accept God's amazing grace, forgiveness and cleansing. When God forgives, He forgets — but often we don't forgive ourselves or forget our sins. Satan is a master at using the memory of past sins to rob us of inner joy, peace and cleansing. Let me ask you an important question: If you confess your sins to God, and God forgets those sins when he forgives them, who is the one responsible for bringing them up again later? Why, Satan is, of course! As soon as Satan attempts to bring to your mind your already confessed sins, simply rebuke him and thank God for His loving grace and forgiveness!

If you have a difficult time accepting God's forgiveness, I would invite you to try an assignment I often use very effectively in counseling. Simply write on a piece of paper all your sins that trouble you or cause you guilt. Confess them in prayer to God at that time. Put the piece of paper in a little box and bury it outside in the ground. It may even help to put a small tombstone on the burial site. Then thank God that those sins are dead and buried (as Romans 6:2-18 teaches), and that they have been forgiven and forgotten.

Try it. It works because it is God's plan for what to do when you don't know what to do about guilt!

TALKING BACK

1. The Bible says, "be sure your sin will find you out." How does sin find us out?

2. How is the conscience "seared," or deadened, so that one feels little or no guilt? What are the consequences of such deadening of the conscience?

3. Discuss some ways people attempt to relieve their guilt . How do you seek to relieve your guilt?

4. How can Satan use your past to ruin your future?

5. Have you had problems forgiving yourself for any sin from the past? What have you learned from this lesson about releasing guilt and accepting forgiveness?

EXERCISING YOUR FAITH

1. Carry out the "sin burial" exercise mentioned near the end of this chapter. If necessary, erect a small tombstone on the burial site to remind you that those sins are forgiven and forgotten by God.

2. Make a list of those things that have caused you to feel guilty and with which you would like God's help. Spend some time praying for God to give you the strength to correct any unresolved situations. Also ask God to help you learn to forgive yourself.

4

REJECTION

I was 16 years old and in love. The only problem was that she didn't know it; in fact, I wasn't even sure she had ever noticed me. Finally, I worked up enough courage to ask her out for a date to the Tennessee State Fair. There was a long pause on the phone, and then she finally responded, "I can't go. I just don't have anything to wear."

They say that time heals all wounds, but that was one wound of rejection that was very difficult to forget. I knew it was rejection because her father was very wealthy, certainly wealthy enough to make sure she had something appropriate to wear ... and because I had spoken to her earlier that day at school and am quite certain she was wearing something then!

The fear of rejection is one of the most basic and common fears known to man. "Rejection" means, "to refuse acceptance, or recognition; to discard; to cast away as worthless." Have you ever been refused acceptance by an individual or a group of people? Have you ever felt discarded? Have you ever felt like someone wanted to make you feel worthless? If so, you know the deep pain of rejection.

Some time ago a poll was taken among a group of high school students with the question, "What do you most desire in life?" A strong majority of those students said they wanted to be popular, to be accepted. In other words, they didn't want to experience rejection. That same desire is inherent in nearly all of us, regardless of our age.

REASONS WE FEEL REJECTED

Occasional feelings of rejection are quite common. The problem comes when we allow these feelings to dominate and control our personality. We can even become so accustomed to rejection that we start bringing it on ourselves. Let's look at some common reasons we may feel rejected.

The most obvious reason is when we have been refused acceptance or turned away by others. We all have a very basic need to be loved and accepted. These feelings can begin very early for the child who fears rejection by his parents, and this fear of rejection intensifies during the teen years when peer acceptance is so important. Rejection, whether real or perceived, during these years can be difficult to cope with and can be a root cause of teenage depression.

Comparing ourselves with someone who appears strong in an area where we feel weak can also cause feelings of rejection. This is a particularly unfair comparison since you may not be aware of the other person's weaknesses. This unequal comparison can contribute to your own feelings of rejection. Such comparisons are unhealthy and are usually unfair.

Some feel rejected because they have fewer material possessions than others. We must understand that our sense of worth and value should never be based upon earthly possessions. You are somebody, not because of what you have but because of who you are.

Feeling deprived of love is another basic reason for feeling rejected. We all need to be loved unconditionally. When one perceives that he is not really loved, or that he is loved only if he performs well or succeeds, he is being set up for rejection.

These are just a few of the most common reasons we may sometimes feel rejected. Before leaving this thought, we should also understand that some rejection may be good for us, even if we don't understand it at the time. This occurs when we are rejected by the world because we have taken a stand for Jesus. Like the young man Daniel, who "resolved not to defile himself" (Daniel 1:8), we may be rejected, mocked, laughed at or scorned when we choose God's way over the ways of the world or Satan. When facing this kind of rejection, it is important for us to remember that "God and I make a majority." Like Daniel, the faithful will be victorious ultimately!

CHRISTIAN CHARACTER TRAITS

Another reason we may possibly feel rejected is because we have never mastered the knack of being popular or accepted. Being accepted by others usually can be accomplished by applying some basic Christian character traits to your life. The most basic of those traits is a sincere interest in and love for people. It is extremely difficult for a person to reject you when you are loving and kind toward him.

If you are interested in being accepted or liked, consider some Christian traits you would do well to develop:

Love — A sincere and genuine love for others is essential to being liked or accepted. If you concentrate on loving others instead of being loved, you will find acceptance. Try to acquire humorist Will Rogers' philosophy: "I never met a man I didn't like."

Friendliness — A smile is contagious, and the whole world needs a friend. Solomon wrote, "A man that hath friends must show himself friendly" (Proverbs 18:24 KJV).

Kindness — Arrogance and thoughtlessness do not help to achieve acceptance from other people. Someone has said, "Be nice and kind to everybody because everybody is having a hard time." Kindness can help lighten someone else's load, and help you receive acceptance at the same time.

Dependability — Many people experience rejection from others because they are not dependable and cannot be trusted to do what they say. Obtain a reputation of doing more than is expected. A willingness to cooperate with others and "go the second mile" are virtues that will help you to be accepted and respected.

Humility — The show-off, loud-mouthed, egotistical know-it-all will always have trouble being accepted. Instead, follow Paul's advice to "be completely humble and gentle; be patient, bearing with one another in love" (Ephesians 4:2). Humility is the ability of knowing how to feel neither inferior nor superior to others.

These are just a few of the character traits that will help you to be accepted by others — but you need to beware of a hidden danger. A person can have such a strong desire to be accepted by others that he compromises his convictions. Acceptance from friends or peers is not so important as to sacrifice your basic beliefs or your integrity. Again we call upon the wisdom of Paul: "Do not conform any longer to the pattern of this world, but be transformed by the renewing of your mind. Then you will be able to test and approve what God's will is — his good, pleasing and perfect will" (Romans 12:2). Always remember that while acceptance from friends is good, the Lord is better!

The worst rejection anyone could ever experience is rejection from God. Hell is the ultimate rejection, but God does not want to reject people. To avoid that terrible punishment, God instead rejected His Son, Jesus Christ, allowing Him to be crucified for our redemption.

If anyone ever knew the meaning of rejection it was our Lord and Savior, Jesus Christ. He was the Son of God. He was perfect and sinless. He was kind and compassionate. He never did an evil deed. He never hurt anyone. If anyone ever deserved to be accepted, it was Jesus Christ!

Yet, Jesus was not accepted; in fact, He experienced total rejection. Isaiah 53:3 reads, "He was despised and rejected by men, a man of sorrows, and familiar with suffering. Like one from whom men hide their faces he was despised, and we esteemed him not." He was beaten (Matthew 27:26); He was mocked (Matthew 27:28-29); He was spit upon and slapped (Matthew 27:30); and, finally, He was crucified. He certainly did not deserve any of the sufferings He endured. If anyone ever knew the meaning of rejection, it was Jesus.

Jesus is best able to help us learn the true meaning of acceptance. Jesus has said to us, "Come to me, all you who are weary and burdened, and I will give you rest" (Matthew 11:28). One thing is certain: Although you may sometimes feel that others have rejected you, Jesus is a friend who will *never* reject you! He said, "Surely I am with you always, to the very end of the age" (Matthew 28:20).

WHAT TO DO

You can overcome rejection! Consider these important truths that will help you towards this goal:

1. *God loves you and accepts you.* God does not reject you. Jesus said, "Whoever comes to me I will never drive away" (John 6:37). God loves you, cares for you, and accepts you just as you are. The Bible tells us that the Christian is an adopted and accepted child of God (Ephesians 1:5-6). Accept God's love and claim His acceptance.

2. *Stop rejecting yourself, and start accepting yourself.* Some rejection is self-imposed. It is not wrong to like yourself (See Leviticus 19:18; Matthew 22:39; James 2:8). Someone once said, "I don't want you loving me like you love yourself because I couldn't stand the hate." You are a child of God, a co-heir with Jesus (Romans 8:17), worthy of being accepted — so act like it!

3. *Realize that people often are not rejecting you as a person but are rather rejecting an attitude or an action.* Suppose that one time your parents were so frustrated with your behavior that they told you that you weren't worth anything — you might well feel rejected by them. That would never be the right thing for them to say, but they are not perfect either. In this situation your parents were not really rejecting you, but your behavior. Parents usually want what is best for their children, and caring parents do not intentionally attempt to destroy their children by rejecting them. If you feel rejection from your parents, talk it out with them and forgive them. Whether the rejection you feel is from parents or others, recognize that the rejection may be of a harmful action or attitude — not you.

4. Refuse to allow an apparent rejection by others to get you down. If someone rejects you, let it be the other person's problem, not yours. Since God will never reject you, you shouldn't accept rejection from others. When the young shepherd boy David was preparing to fight Goliath, his older brother put him down in front of others (1 Samuel 17:28). David simply "turned away to someone else" (1 Samuel 17:30), meaning that he refused to let his brother's rejection get him down. Instead, he sought out those who would accept him. You can do that, too, by simply refusing to allow rejection to discourage you, and by turning to those who accept and love you.

5. Finally, realize that you can control how you are affected by rejection. Eleanor Roosevelt said, "No one can make you feel inferior without your consent." You control how you respond to rejection and other negative circumstances.

A story is told about a man who met a beggar. The man said, "God give you a good day, my friend."

"I thank God," said the beggar, "I have never had a bad one."

"God give you a happy life, my friend," said the man.

"I thank God," answered the beggar, "I have never been unhappy."

"What do you mean?" asked the man.

"Well," said the beggar, "when it is fine, I thank God; when it rains, I thank God; when I have plenty, I thank God; when I am hungry, I thank God; and since God's will is my will, and whatever pleases Him pleases me, why should I say I am unhappy when I am not?"

The man looked at the beggar with astonishment and said, "Who are you?"

"I am a king," he replied.

"Where is your kingdom?" the man asked.

"In my heart," the beggar answered quietly.

Jesus will give you that unshakable kingdom of the heart that will overcome rejection if you allow Him to do so.

TALKING BACK

1. Have you ever compromised your beliefs or values in order to avoid the risk of being rejected? How?

2. Why do you think the desire to be accepted is so strong? Why do we fear rejection?

3. At what times might rejection be good for us?

4. Why is Jesus best able to help us cope with rejection? What can we learn from Jesus about rejection?

5. Discuss the statement, "No one can make you feel inferior without you consent."

EXERCISING YOUR FAITH

1. Write a letter to me — a "Dear Randy" letter. Describe a problem with rejection you are having, or have had, and ask my advice. Then, answer your own letter. Write a letter back to yourself about how to handle the rejection you are feeling.

2. Look for someone who is experiencing rejection. I'm confident you can identify someone at school or church. Reach out to that person with the love of God — give them a smile, write them a note, or let them know you care in some other way.

PRESSURE

Susan was a bright and beautiful 16-year-old girl. A class leader and cheerleader at her high school, she was multi-talented and had many interests. On the outside she appeared to have it all — but on the inside she was about ready to crack up. Through her tears she said to me, "I don't know what to do. I feel pressure everywhere I turn. I feel pressure at home with my parents. I feel pressure at school. I feel pressured by my friends. I don't know how much longer I can take it."

Pressure affects everyone, but people handle pressure differently. What do you do when you feel too much pressure? Some people cry. Others yell, scream or snap at people. Still others drink, smoke, take drugs or overeat. Some even tear their hair out. But none of these responses do any good. A century before the time of Christ, the philosopher Cicero wrote, "It is no use tearing thy hair out in grief. Thy baldness will not lessen thy sorrow." Neither will thy temper, thy drunkenness or thy withdrawal!

It is not so much the *presence* of pressure in our lives that causes problems, but how we *handle* pressure that will determine whether we "make it or break it."

If I were not a preacher, I would probably be a coach. I had the pleasure of coaching a little football and basketball a few years ago, and I always thought the key to success was putting pressure on the other team. In basketball, my teams played a pressure defense taught by Indiana coach Bob Knight. Our pressure defense worked like this:

- An offensive player who is dribbling the ball is trapped by two defensive players, forcing him to pick up the ball and stop his dribble.

- The closest defensive player to the man with the ball starts waving his arms and yells, "Pressure!", knowing that the offensive player has used up his right to dribble.

- This triggers a reaction from the other four defensive players, who get between their man and the ball, cutting off all the passing lanes for the poor guy with the ball. Sometimes our players on the bench would get into the act and scream, "Pressure!"

What happened? It depended largely upon what the player with the ball was made of. Many players simply couldn't take the pressure and would throw the ball away, and some would freeze and stand there until the referee called a jump ball.

TOO MUCH PRESSURE

Many Christians today seem to act like a pressure defense has been thrown up all around them. They simply do not seem to be able to respond to any type of pressure and, as a result, they often feel defeated by life. It doesn't have to be that way!

Why was Susan feeling so much pressure? Why do you, perhaps, feel too pressured from time? Let's look at some common causes of teen pressures:

Competition to succeed — Competition is not all bad. It can challenge us to discover and use our talents, motivate us and provide needed entertainment. But competition can also destroy. It can cause people to drive themselves unmercifully and subject themselves to severe pressure and stress. Unchecked, it can wear one down physically, emotionally, mentally and even spiritually. The teen who feels he or she must excel academically, athletically, socially and in every other way, can be in danger of too much pressure.

Unrealistic goals — If you view yourself as Superman or Wonder Woman, you may be setting yourself up for a pressure-induced fall. When we set unrealistic goals for ourselves, we feel much pressure as obstacles get in the way of our success. Certainly, we should set goals, but we also should: 1. be sure they are realistic; and 2. surrender our plans and goals to God, making sure they are His plans and goals for us.

Time demands — One of the greatest pressures on busy teens is a lack of time. I know that in Susan's case, she goes to school, is involved in several extracurricular activities at school, works a job, is very active in the church youth group, and is active socially — and then she wonders why she feels so pressured? Trying to do too much in too little time can create an enormous amount of stress in our lives.

Bad habits — When a habit has become addictive to the point that you feel unable to shake it or control it, pressure or stress will result. Some bad habits (drug abuse, alcohol abuse, sexual immorality, lying, stealing, etc.) put one under constant pressure and can be so destructive that they threaten to shorten your life and damage your relationship with your family and friends.

Irresponsibility — Some pressure is self-induced stress caused by our own mismanagement of our lifestyle. For instance, procrastination leads to self-induced pressure. At the opposite end of the spectrum, over scheduling yourself can keep you feeling frustrated and pressured all day long.

Guilt — Unresolved guilt over sinful actions, attitudes or thoughts can be the source of emotional pressure. When you feel such pressure, face your sin, confess it, correct it and forget it (see Chapter 3). Trying to ignore sin only increases your pressure; following God's instructions will eliminate emotional stresses.

Certainly, these are not all of the causes of teenage pressure, but they seem to be the major ones. When I think of pressure, I am reminded of a fly that was trapped inside my car recently. Trying desperately to get out, the fly would buzz around frantically and then dart toward the windows, only to be knocked down repeatedly by the clear, raised window panes. That little fly reminded me of a lot of people who have no real inner faith to fall back on when they feel pressured. As a result, they just "buzz around," keep "hitting the glass" and the pressure continues to mount until they either crack up or give up.

When I let the windowpane down, the fly dashed toward its freedom and, I suppose, was relieved of its frustration. How can we let the window panes down in our lives and escape some of our destructive pressures?

Before I share some practical suggestions for reducing pressures, consider this excellent advice from the Alcoholics Anonymous organization, one of the programs of the Hazeldon Foundation in Center City, Minn.:

JUST FOR TODAY

Just for today, I will live through the next 12 hours and not
  tackle my whole life's problems at once.
Just for today, I will improve my mind.
I will learn something useful.
I will read something that requires effort, thought and con-
  centration.
Just for today, I will be agreeable.
I will look my best.
Speak in a well-modulated voice,
be courteous and considerate.
Just for today, I will not find fault
with friend, relative or colleague.
I won't try to change or improve anyone but myself.
Just for today, I will have a program.

I might not follow it exactly, but I will have it.

I will save myself from two enemies: hurry and indecision.

Just for today, I will exercise my character in three ways.

I will do a good turn and keep it secret.

If anyone finds out, it won't count.

Just for today, I will do two things I don't want to do, just
for exercise.

Just for today, I will be unafraid.

Especially will I be unafraid to enjoy what is beautiful

and believe that as I give to the world,

the world will give to me,

living one day at a time.

(From *Twenty Four Hours A Day*; copyright 1975 by Hazeldon Foundation, Center City, Minn. Reprinted by permission.)

WHAT TO DO

Taking this advice will go a long way toward relieving pressure and stress. Now, for a few biblical and practical suggestions on what to do about pressure:

1. Take an honest look at yourself. We must understand that we can't do everything, so we ought not feel stressed when everything we plan or attempt doesn't turn out just right. Don't be just a "human doing" — be a human being!

2. Release your pressures through prayer. Peter wrote, "Cast all your anxiety on him because he cares for you" (1 Peter 5:7). The great hymn "What a Friend We Have in Jesus" says it well:

What a Friend we have in Jesus,
All our sins and griefs to bear;
What a privilege to carry
Everything to God in prayer.

When we take our pressures to the Lord in prayer, we find great peace and power: "Do not be anxious about anything, but in everything, by prayer and petition, with thanksgiving, present your requests to God. And the peace of God, which transcends all understanding, will guard your hearts and your minds in Christ Jesus" (Philippians 4:6-7). When pressure strikes your life, ask for God's help, trust Him to give it, do your best, and leave the rest to Him!

3. Lean on good friends for encouragement and support. One way to reduce pressure is to talk it out with a good friend or respected leader (youth minister or worker, minister, teacher, coach, counselor, etc.). We are to "carry each other's burdens" (Galatians 6:2), "bearing with one another in love" (Ephesians 4:2). When we share our burdens with a friend, two good things can happen: a. We can find help in dealing with our burdens and pressures; b. We give another person the opportunity and privilege of serving and being a blessing.

4. Make time for effective planning of your activities and quiet meditation. Too many of us are always in a hurry. We are impatient people who do not like planning or waiting. But planning our activities to allow time for prayer, meditation, thinking and rest can help release some of our pressures. The French philosopher Blaise Pascal once wrote, "All the evils of life have fallen upon us because men will not sit quietly in a room. We have got to be doing something, going somewhere, or talking to someone." Ouch! Such a lifestyle is a far cry from the admonition of Psalm 46:10: "Be still, and know that I am God."

5. Practice living one day at a time. Adopt the attitude of King David: "This is the day the Lord has made; let us rejoice and be glad in it" (Psalm 118:24). The next 24 hours are the most important 24 hours that God allows you to live. Concentrate on appreciating and enjoying them.

6. Examine whether or not your schedule is God's schedule. Your schedule is not His schedule if it is crushing you. Some pressure can be good for us, motivating and challenging us to reach our potentials. Someone has said, "A tire without pressure is flat and doesn't do its job — and neither do people." This is true, but we cannot continually go from one pressure-packed crisis to another without cracking. Is your schedule the schedule God would have for you?

The next time you feel like the entire Chicago Bears defense has surrounded you and is pressuring you into submission, remember this: There is One who is greater than all of the pressures of life. Lean on Him!

TALKING BACK

1. Do you know anyone like Susan? What would have been your advice to Susan?

2. What do you do when you feel too much pressure? What are some healthy and unhealthy ways to respond to pressure?

3. What kinds of things cause you to feel too much pressure? Discuss some of the common causes of pressure or stress among teens.

4. What is the difference between a "human being" and a "human doing"?

5. Read though the six practical suggestions for dealing with pressure in the lesson. Which of the suggestions have you tried? Which of the suggestions do you need to try?

EXERCISING YOUR FAITH

1. Read "Just For Today" every day this week. Pray that God will help you to internalize this good counsel.

2. Hold your hand close to a match, lighter, stove or other flame. Let it remind you of the heat you feel because of pressure. Before your hand burns, dip it in cool water. Allow this exercise to remind you to rely on God to deliver you from the fire of pressure and keep you cool under pressure.

PARENTS

F irst of all, I have a confession to make about this chapter: I didn't intend to write it. It was not on my original list of chapter topics.

Eight of our teenagers at my home congregation are helping me with this book by evaluating each chapter and making recommendations. I asked them, "What chapter suggestions do you have?" Four of them wrote back, "My relationship with my parents." Then a youth minister friend informed me that when he asked his youth group to list the problems that bothered them most, more than half of them put "getting along with my parents" as first or second on the list. I think it deserves its own chapter.

Unbearable family tensions and fights with parents are a major cause of teenage runaways. Most runaways will run anywhere. They are more interested in running *from* than *to* any specific location:

> Lisa fits all the statistics. She is 14 years old. She left home to get away from what she perceived to be intolerable family conditions. She had quarreled constantly with her parents about nearly everything until the tension became unbearable. She left her comfortable middle-class home for California, taking a bus part of the way and hitch-hiking the remainder.

Like nearly all the 20,000 runaways who flock yearly to Los Angeles, Lisa entered the city without a penny or a friend. She spent nearly three weeks sleeping in parks and in the doorways of stores. She begged money for food and, at times, ate out of garbage pails. At last, exhausted and defeated, Lisa turned herself in to the police and was returned to her family.

"Lisa's case is quite common," stated the social worker in charge of Lisa's case. "She thought the tension between herself and her parents was intolerable. Lacking alternatives to deal constructively with that tension, she did what she thought was the only thing she could do to escape it. She split."

Running away is only one way some teens seek to resolve a bad relationship with their parents. On the one hand, most of us love our parents, but on the other hand, we often harbor feelings of anger, resentment and frustration toward them. Even though parents love their children, they often have those same feelings toward their children.

WHAT TO DO

What do you do when you don't know what to do about your relationship with your parents? Maybe the following bits of advice can be helpful:

1. *Give your parents the benefit of the doubt.* Most parents today are confused about how to relate to you. They have forgotten what it was like to be a teenager, and even if they do remember, the pressures on teens today are different than what they faced. Also, parents are a bit nervous, having read or heard about drug abuse, teenage alcoholism, the increase in sexually transmitted diseases, and the like. They are probably more afraid of your rejecting them as parents than you are afraid of their rejecting you as children.

The thought of losing one's kids is frightening to most parents.

Your parents' pressures may be many — financial, job, future, aging relatives, age creeping up on them, etc. — give them the benefit of the doubt. The next time you complain that they don't understand you, ask yourself honestly, "Have I tried to understand them?" Fairness demands that it work both ways.

2. *Learn to forgive your parents.* No one would suggest that parents are perfect. They make mistakes like everyone else. But holding anger or resentment against them and withholding forgiveness will not help you or them. Ask yourself, "What will be accomplished by continuing to focus on my parents' faults and refusing to forgive them?" Nothing good. Ephesians 4:26-27 reads, "'In your anger do not sin': Do not let the sun go down while you are still angry, and do not give the devil a foothold." When you feel anger, deal with it quickly and forgive. Don't let even one day pass without resolving your anger, or you will be giving Satan a "foothold" to defeat you. Forgive!

3. *Avoid meeting rejection with rejection.* If you feel rejection from your parents, do not meet those feelings with more rejection; instead counter them by expressing love. In the mid-1970s singer-songwriter Harry Chapin recorded "Cat's In The Cradle" — a song emphasizing the foolishness of parents and children rejecting one another. In the song, a boy keeps asking for his father's attention, but the father is too busy. Still the boy wants to grow up to be like his father. By the end of the song, the boy is grown and the father is asking for attention — but the son is too busy for his father, who laments:

> And as I hung up the phone, it occurred to me,
> He'd grown up just like me — my boy was just like me.

We must learn not to meet rejection with rejection, but to meet rejection with love.

4. *Believe the Word of God concerning your relationship with your parents.* Consider what Scripture says is your obligation to your parents:

"Children, obey your parents in the Lord, for this is right. 'Honor your father and mother' — which is the first commandment with a promise — 'that it may go well with you and that you may enjoy long life on the earth'" (Ephesians 6:1-3).

"Children, obey your parents in everything, for this pleases the Lord" (Colossians 3:20).

"A wise son heeds his father's instruction, but a mocker does not listen to rebuke" (Proverbs 13:1).

Obeying our parents may not always be easy, but in the long run it is the best choice because God's Word demands it. Obeying our parents pleases God, it is the right thing to do and, although we may not understand it at the time, it is best for us.

5. Earn your parents' trust. Teenagers need strong "roots" and stability, but at the same time, they need some "wings" with which to fly and exert some independence. The best way to get your wings from your parents is to show them that you are trustworthy. There are many ways that you can communicate the message, "I can be trusted" to your parents (accept responsibilities, follow directions, maintain proper attitudes, don't show disrespect, don't be sneaky, etc.). Tell your parents that you can be trusted, and then prove it with your actions and attitudes.

6 Practice the art of good communication with your parents. We need to build bridges instead of barriers in our communication. What are some of the barriers to effective teen-parent communication?

- Lying
- Anger
- Silence
- Shouting
- Misinterpretation
- Quarreling
- Bitterness
- Rejection
- Avoidance
- Not listening

Any of these can hinder effective communication and lead to a breakdown in relationships.

Consider a few practical suggestions for building communication bridges to your parents:

Choose an appropriate time and place to talk. Times of stress and pressure are not the best times to confront issues of importance.

Be direct but gentle. Remember that words can hurt deeply. If you disagree with them, try an approach like this: "I'm going to do what you've asked, but it would help if I could understand what your reason is, or why this is important."

Always tell the truth. Lying creates distrust. Honest communication depends upon honest conversation. Telling the truth builds bridges, while lying builds barriers.

"A gentle answer turns away wrath, but a harsh word stirs up anger" (Proverbs 15:1). Remembering this biblical counsel during a conversation is difficult, but if we can remember it and practice it, we will see benefits.

Deal with problems before they get too big. Families in stress often shut down their communication either by not acknowledging a problem or refusing to deal with it. When the problem finally becomes a crisis, panic sets in and communication is sour. Talk out problems calmly, reasonably and rationally before they get out of hand.

Use the "Serenity Prayer" as a guide in communication:

God grant me the serenity to accept the things I
cannot change, the courage to change the things
I can, and the wisdom to know the difference.

Control what you can control, which is yourself. You cannot control or change your parents. You may try hard to communicate better and find that your parents, for whatever reasons, are not responding to your efforts at improvement. Just do your best — that is all God would ask and expect of you. Accept what you cannot change, and change for the better what you can change. Such an attitude will help you, even if your parents never respond.

7. *Finally, and most importantly, love your parents.* I know that sounds corny, but it is so important. The apostle Peter wrote, "Above all, love each other deeply, because love covers over a multitude of sins" (1 Peter 4:8). True love will overcome any obstacle. "It always protects, always trusts, always hopes, always perseveres. Love never fails" (1 Corinthians 13:7-8).

My father passed away in June 1989 after a lengthy illness. Although we lived hundreds of miles apart, we tried to talk on the phone often. The night before he died, I was talking to him on the phone, and the last words I ever spoke to him were, "I love you." I'm glad I had that opportunity — many don't. While you can express love for your parents, do it!

Improving your relationship with your parents takes time and effort, but it is worth it. And remember, someday you may be the parent of a teenager yourself, so what you learn and practice now could really help you later!

TALKING BACK

1. To "honor my father and mother" (Ephesians 6:1-3) means ...

2. In what ways do you give your parents the benefit of the doubt? In what ways do your parents give you the benefit of the doubt?

3. Describe what you think it means that teenagers need "roots" and "wings."

4. What are some of the barriers to effective communication between you and your parents? Discuss some ways to overcome these barriers.

5. Why is it so important that you learn to love your parents?

EXERCISING YOUR FAITH

1. Draw up a Parent Report Card (A-Excellent: B-Above Average; C-Average; D-Below Average; F-Failing). Grade your relationship with your parents in these key areas:
   _____ Loving My Parents
   _____ Honoring My Parents
   _____ Obeying My Parents
   _____ Communicating with My Parents
   _____ Understanding My Parents
   _____ Learning My Parents' Values

   Which grade are you the most dissatisfied with? What can you do about it?

2. Write a letter to your parents expressing your love and appreciation for them. Go ahead — it will shock them!

NEGATIVE ATTITUDES

 high school teacher once had his class conduct an experiment with "jumping fleas." The students put hundreds of fleas on a table and observed how high the fleas jumped. Then they put the fleas in a glass jar with a top on it. The fleas continually jumped up and down, but could go no higher than the top because they would hit the lid of the jar. After a while the lid was lifted, but the fleas continued to jump to the same height, as if the lid were still in place. They were limited in how high they could jump by what they thought was there — not by their actual limit!

Many people today have put lids on their minds and refuse to believe that they can jump higher and higher. It is alarming to note how many people refuse to accept any real challenge and are content to be just average, or even below average.

Centuries ago the wise man Solomon wrote that as a man "thinketh in his heart, so is he" (Proverbs 23:7 KJV). World-renowned psychiatrist Dr. Karl Menninger has said, "Attitudes are more important than facts," and he is right. To a great degree, the success or failure one has in life is determined by one's attitudes or thoughts. Radio commentator Paul Harvey has told a story that vividly illustrates this truth:

Several years ago there was a rash of airplane hijackings in the United States, particularly out of the Miami airport. One such plane was hijacked out of Miami on its way to New York. The hijacker ordered, "Turn the plane around and head for Havana, Cuba." The pilot could tell the man was serious and desperate, so he did what the hijacker said.

But a strange thing happened. When the gunman tried to intimidate the passengers, they laughed. They were loose and carefree all the way to Havana. They laughed while the plane was on the ground and while tense negotiations were going on between the American and Cuban authorities. They turned the whole experience into a big party.

Only one man other than the hijacker and the pilot was not laughing. He didn't get the joke. In fact, he was worried that the hijacker would react violently to the laughter of the passengers. His name? Allen Funt, long-time host of the TV show "Candid Camera," which highlights pranks and practical jokes. When the other passengers saw Allen Funt was on the plane, they assumed the hijacking was all a prank. They were waiting for someone to say, "Surprise. You're on Candid Camera!"

It wasn't a prank. But because the passengers thought it was, they relaxed and had a good time.

Again, it is usually true that "attitudes are more important than facts." As Solomon wrote, you are what you think. Fill your mind with negative thoughts and attitudes, and you will be a negative person. On the other hand, fill your mind with positive thoughts and attitudes, and you will reap the benefits of being a positive person (Philippians 4:8).

THE ORIGINAL POSITIVE THINKER

You may not realize it, but the Bible was the original positive thinking manual, and God was the original Positive Thinker. Consider some biblical examples of great men of God who were positive thinkers. Of course, faith was primary to their spiritual success, but they had to be positive minded as well. In Scripture, faith and positive thinking go hand in hand, just as a lack of faith and negative thinking go hand in hand.

Noah — It took great faith and a positive frame of mind for Noah to build an ark before the flood came. He spent decades preaching that God would send a flood and built the ark, and no one outside his family believed him (Genesis 5-6).

Gideon — This great positive thinker led a small army of just 300 men into battle against a Midianite army that was as numerous as "grasshoppers." Yet, God gave them the victory because of their positive faith and obedience (Judges 7).

Joshua and Caleb — These mighty men of faith brought back a positive report as spies on the land of Canaan. They said, "We should go up and take possession of the land, for we can certainly do it." Ten other spies gave a negative report: "We can't attack those people; they are stronger than we are." The people believed the negative reports and, as a result, all adults over the age of 20 were denied entrance to the Promised Land, except for Joshua and Caleb, who God allowed to enter because of their positive faith (Numbers 13-14).

David — This young shepherd boy went into the battle against the giant soldier, Goliath. It seemed like impossible odds for David, but his positive faith caused God to give him the victory (1 Samuel 17).

Paul — Despite his having to overcome numerous obstacles (2 Corinthians 11:23-28), Paul maintained a positive faith that allowed him to say, "I can do everything through him who gives me strength" (Philippians 4:13).

If you say "I can" with Paul, you will get much more done than if you are constantly saying, "I can't." Do not allow obstacles to build up in your mind. Learn to minimize rather than maximize obstacles.

Let's contrast the benefits of a positive attitude with the obstacles of a negative attitude:

POSITIVE ATTITUDE	NEGATIVE ATTITUDE
1. Your "I can" attitude and your faith will help you to plow through obstacles that you never dreamed possible.	1. Your negative attitude will be a tool of the Devil, used to produce a defeatist lifestyle.
2. You will make friends easily and keep them, for people enjoy being around positive, upbeat, encouraging people.	2. You will have difficulty making and keeping friends, for negative thoughts and attitudes drag other people down.
3. Your self-image and self-confidence will improve and will help make you an achiever.	3. You will be trapped in "poor-little-ol'-me" thinking and will most likely fail more than achieve.
4. You will see a silver lining in every cloud. You will be able to see the good in a bad situation. You will be able to see the potential for good in people. You will see an opportunity in every problem.	4. You will see a thorn in every rose bush. You will look for the bad in people rather than the good. You will see a problem in every opportunity.
5. You will develop a habit of doing things right. Good habits tend to spread.	5. You will be satisfied with mediocrity. Bad habits tend to spread.

What a shame when a good future is ruined through the tragic consequences of negative thinking or a negative attitude! How many people have been stopped short of progress because they had an "I can't" attitude? The next time you are tempted to say, "I can't," stop for a moment and consider if what you really mean is, "I won't!"

This marvelous poem has inspired many people to think positive thoughts and cultivate a positive attitude:

> If you think you are beaten, you are;
> If you think you dare not, you don't;
> If you want to win, but you think you can't,
> It's almost a cinch you won't.

If you think you'll lose, you're lost;
For out in the world we find
Success begins with a fellow's will;
It's all in a state of mind.

Life's battles don't always go
To the stronger and faster man,
But sooner or later the man who wins,
Is the man who thinks he can!

WHAT TO DO

How can you cultivate a positive attitude? What can you do about negative attitudes? Here are a few suggestions:

1. Believe that God has given you the right and ability to control your own mind. God's Word promises that negative attitudes can be changed to positive attitudes. Ephesians 4:23 teaches that we can "be made new in the attitude of your minds." And Romans 12:2 reads, "Do not conform any longer to the pattern of this world, but be transformed by the renewing of your mind." These passages of Scripture, and many others, teach that God has given us the power to choose our own attitudes and thoughts.

2. Learn how to replace negative thoughts and attitudes with positive ones. Whenever you begin to experience negative thoughts or attitudes, simply interrupt them and replace them with some alternative thinking about positive things. For every negative attitude there is a positive attitude that can be consciously chosen by you to replace it. For instance, replace worry with faith, replace guilt with forgiveness, replace grumbling with gratitude, replace hatred with love. This thought replacement requires discipline and repetition, but it really works. Try it — you'll like it!

3. Concentrate on looking for the positive, and you will find it. You see what you want to see, or what you are prepared to see, in another person or situation. If you look for the negative in almost any person or situation, you will find it. On the other hand, if you look for the positive, you will find it. A person who exhibits positive attitudes does not refuse to see the negative; he simply refuses to dwell on it. Consider the story of the two shoe salesmen in Africa. One wrote to his boss, "No market here. No one even wears shoes." The other salesman optimistically wrote the boss, "The market here is unlimited! No one has shoes over here!" The difference? One salesman had negative thoughts and attitudes and was looking for the negative — that's what he found. The other salesman had a positive attitude and was looking for the positive, so that's what he found.

4. Practice the spiritual discipline of positive praying. Developing a positive attitude is great, but positive praying is even greater and more powerful. Why? Because positive thinking challenges man, and every man has his limitations. But positive praying challenges God, and He has no limitations! Jesus said, "Ask and it will be given to you; seek and you will find; knock and the door will be opened to you. For everyone who asks receives; he who seeks finds; and to him who knocks, the door will be opened" (Matthew 7:7-8). Praying with faith produces amazing results (Matthew 17:20; James 5:16; Mark 11:22-24; Psalm 81:10; Jeremiah 33:3). Someone has said, "Great men are ordinary people who just will not give up hope. And what is hope? It is Holding On, Praying Expectantly." That is positive praying, which will help you develop a positive attitude, the "attitude of Christ Jesus" (Philippians 2:5).

5. Above all, don't quit — don't give in to negative attitudes. Winners never quit, and quitters never win. There was once a man who had the following record of failures:

> In 1831 he failed in a business venture.
> In 1832 he lost a bid for the legislature.
> In 1833 he failed in another business.
> In 1836 he had a nervous breakdown.
> In 1840 he was defeated for Congress.
> In 1846 he was elected to Congress.
> In 1848 he was defeated in a re-election attempt to Congress.

In 1856 he was defeated for vice president of the United States.
In 1858 he was defeated for Senate.
But in 1860 he was elected to the highest office in America,
the presidency of the United States — and he has been
regarded as one of our nation's finest presidents — Abraham Lincoln was his name. The key to his success was
his "never-give-up" attitude.

Ralph Waldo Emerson wrote, "The hero is no braver than the
ordinary man, but he is brave five minutes longer." Don't quit —
success may be only five minutes away!

In his book *Life Is Tremendous*, Charlie Jones relates this story:

Once a cranky grandpa lay down to take a nap. To have a
little fun with him, his grandson put some limburger cheese
on his mustache under his nose. Grandpa awoke with a snort,
charged out of the bedroom and shouted, "This room stinks!"
As he went through the house, he yelled, "This whole house
stinks!" He charged out onto the porch and shouted, "The
whole world stinks!" The truth was, it was Grandpa who
stunk! The problem was right under his own nose!

Most of the time when we begin to feel like things stink, the
problem is with ourselves. We have allowed negative attitudes to
alter our perception of life. If we will then change our negative
attitudes and thoughts to positive ones, we can change the world.

Let me challenge you to put Philippians 4:13 into practice in
your life. Memorize it. Repeat it over and over again. Most importantly, believe it!

TALKING BACK

1. Solomon wrote, "As a man thinketh in his heart, so is he." Menniger said, "Attitudes are more important than facts." What do these statements mean?

2. In the lesson, five biblical examples of faith and positive thinking are discussed. Which of these men do you think faced the greatest obstacles to thinking positive?

3. Discuss the difference in attitude between "I can't" and "I won't."

4. How can "thought replacement" help change your attitudes? How can it help in living the Christian life?

5. What is positive praying? Why is it even better than positive thinking?

EXERCISING YOUR FAITH

1. Write a letter to yourself about the kind of person you want to be in the future. Write about attitudes you like in yourself now and attitudes you'd like to change in the near future. Put the letter in a stamped envelope and give it to a trusted friend. Ask your friend to mail it to you in a month so you can check up on yourself.

2. Memorize Philippians 4:13. Repeat it to yourself every time a negative attitude hounds you.

SELF IMAGE

Scattered throughout this chapter are short, capitalized sentences that I want you to really think about and consider when you come to them. The first is: **"GOD LOVES YOU."**

Some time ago several groups of high school students were surveyed with three questions:

1. What would you do to change your appearance to be more acceptable to others?
2. What abilities do you wish that you had that you do not have?
3. Why do you feel inferior, if you feel that you are?

Here is a sampling of their answers to those questions: too fat, too skinny, big nose, no dates, acne, bad voice, wear glasses or contacts, poor hair, bow-legged, uncoordinated, scars, big ears, few friends, no praise and much criticism.

I can identify with those responses. I remember the anguish of pimples breaking out on my face just before the "big date." I know the pain of being a bench-warmer on the high school baseball team. I remember the agony of being turned down for a date. I know how it feels to drive an old jalopy to school when my friends were driving Trans Ams.

Most of us would like to change certain things about ourselves and our appearance — and we may need to make some changes that we have the ability to change. However, we also need to remember this important truth: **"GOD LOVES US JUST THE WAY WE ARE."**

The first and most important step in feeling good about yourself is to recognize that you are created in God's image, and that fact alone makes you very important. God does not love you because you are valuable to Him; you are valuable to Him because He loves you! Problems with our self-image come when we think we are, or are not, worthwhile or valuable for other reasons.

Consider the school athlete. If he fails in a game, he may tell himself that he isn't worth much; if he succeeds in a game, he may base his self-image on the false idea that athletic ability or performance makes one valuable. In either case, he is wrong because he has supposed that his worth as a person depends upon his ability to perform as an athlete. The same principle can be applied to academic achievement, physical appearance, popularity with others, vocation or money.

Our worth is not based on our performance or what we do, but it is based on God's performance and what He did! This means that everybody can be somebody. We can feel good about ourselves if we keep things in a proper perspective and stay in a right relationship with the Lord. **"YOU ARE SPECIAL. YOU ARE IMPORTANT TO GOD."**

WHAT TO DO

Only when we get our sense of self-worth from God and His Word can we have a proper self-image. How can you be certain to get a proper self-image? Remember these four important truths:

1. *Realize that God made you as you are.* Revelation 4:11 reads, "You are worthy, our Lord and God, to receive glory and honor and power, for you created all things, and by your will they were created and have their being." Some would say, "Well, I'm too short" or "I'm too tall." Too short or too tall for what? To accomplish something you may want to do? Maybe. But not to accomplish the purpose for which you were created — and that is far more important. Looking at yourself as a product of God's handiwork makes it less likely that you will focus on what you believe are deficiencies in yourself.

Dr. Karl Barth, one of the greatest theologians of the 20th century, came to the United States to give lectures in 1960. A reporter asked him, "Dr. Barth, what is the most profound thought you have ever had?" What a question! How would this great theologian respond? Dr. Barth replied, "The most profound thought I have ever had is this: Jesus loves me, this I know, for the Bible tells me so!"

He does love you. He made you. Don't buy into Satan's lies that you are worthless and unimportant. The great God of all creation made you and loves you! **"WHO ARE YOU TO NOT LOVE WHAT GOD LOVES?"**

2. God expects you to like yourself because you are created in His image. Genesis 1:27 reads, "So God created man in his own image, in the image of God he created him; male and female he created them." To become like Jesus (which is our goal) is to love what He loves — and He loves you!

The Pharisees once asked Jesus, "What do you think is the greatest commandment of all?" Jesus replied, "'Love the Lord your God with all your heart and with all your soul and with all your mind.' This is the first and greatest commandment. And the second is like it: 'Love your neighbor as yourself'"Matthew 22:37-39).

Jesus knew that if you don't love yourself, it is impossible to love other people. When we realize that it is OK to love ourselves, and realize our worth and value in the sight of God, we will feel much better about ourselves. **"TO LOVE YOURSELF IS TO OBEY JESUS."**

3. Understand that God made you unique. He did not make you to be like anyone else. You are a designer edition! You are not inferior to anyone. Different, yes, but not inferior.

One of the worst crimes you can commit against yourself is to play the comparison game — comparing yourself with another person. God doesn't want you comparing the way He made you with the way He made any other person. Paul wrote, "We do not dare to classify or compare ourselves with some who commend themselves. When they measure themselves by themselves and compare themselves with themselves, they are not wise" (2 Corinthians 10:12).

Everyone was not given the same talent, ability, or even desire and motivation. Comparing yourself to someone who has been given different talents, abilities or drives is an unhealthy thing to do. Such unfair comparisons deflate us, cause intense jealousy, harmful competition, and lead to poor self-image and feelings of inferiority.

You will be a much healthier, happier person if you can learn to accept that you were never made to be just like any other person. Accept yourself for who you are — a designer original, the unique creation of a God who loves you! **"GOD DON'T MAKE NO JUNK!"**

4. Realize that God is still making you, still working on you. His work on you will continue throughout life. In Ephesians 2:10 we read, "For we are God's workmanship, created in Christ Jesus to do good works, which God prepared in advance for us to do." We are God's "workmanship." He will always be working on us to be "conformed to the likeness of his Son" (Romans 8:29).

Perhaps you have seen the bumper sticker, "Be patient with me. God isn't finished with me yet!" There is much truth in that little slogan. Don't be too hard on yourself or get too down on yourself. Allow God the time and opportunity to continue working on you.

Having the love of God in your life is not conditional upon your doing everything perfectly. Many teens suffer needlessly because they are always trying to earn God's acceptance and love — and if they make a mistake, they feel defeated. You don't have to prove anything to God or earn God's love and acceptance. He already loves and accepts you. Believe that. **"YOU CAN BECOME MORE LIKE CHRIST, MORE OF THAT WONDERFUL PERSON GOD CREATED YOU TO BE."**

The things we often believe we need in order to feel good about ourselves and be successful are usually not what we really need. As newspaper columnist Michael Guido wrote, "A sound body, a brilliant mind, a cultural background, a huge amount of money, a wonderful education — none of these guarantee success." Consider, for instance:

> Thomas Edison was deaf and a school drop-out.
> Abraham Lincoln's parents were illiterate.
> Julius Caesar suffered from epilepsy.
> Booker T. Washington was born into slavery.
> Helen Keller, who could not see or hear, graduated with honors from a famous college.
> Theodore Roosevelt was afflicted with asthma as a child .
> The apostle Paul was beaten, tortured, and imprisoned.
> Our Lord Jesus Christ, who was God made flesh, was subjected to human nature and man's abuse and killed unjustly.

"THE FIRST KEY TO SUCCESS IS ACCEPTING WHO YOU ARE AND RECOGNIZING THAT YOU ARE A LOVED CHILD OF GOD."

Evangelist Fred Craddock and his family were vacationing in Gatlinburg, Tenn. While dining in a restaurant overlooking the Smoky Mountains, an older man who seemed to be the owner was moving from table to table speaking to guests. When the old man found out Craddock was a preacher, he said, "I have got a preacher story I need to tell you."

The old man said, "I was born just a few miles from here, just across the mountain. My mother was not married at the time, and the reproach that fell on her fell on me as well. They had a name for me when I started to school, and it was not nice. I can remember going off by myself at recess and at lunchtime because the taunts of my peers cut so deep. What was even worse was going to town with my mother on Saturdays and feeling all those eyes literally piercing through me, and realizing they were asking, 'Whose child is he? I wonder who his father is.'

"When I was about 12, a new preacher came to the little church in our community, and people began to talk about his power and eloquence. I began to go myself, although I always slipped in late and tried to get out early because I was afraid that people would say, 'What is a boy like you doing in a place like this?' But one Sunday, I found myself caught in the crowd, unable to get out the door quickly. As I was waiting there, scared to death, I felt a hand on my shoulder and turned around. There stood the preacher, looking at me with those burning eyes. He said, 'Who are you, son? Whose boy are you?' And I thought to myself, Oh, no, here we go again.

"But then," he said, "a smile of recognition broke across the preacher's face, and he said, 'Wait a minute. I know who you are. I see the family resemblance. You are a son of God!' And with that, he patted me across the rump and said, 'Boy, you've got quite an inheritance. Go and claim it!' That one statement," said the old man, "literally changed my whole life."

By this time, Craddock was totally immersed in the old man's story and asked, "Who are you?"

The old man replied, "Ben Hooper."

Then Craddock remembered the name, and said to himself, "Ben Hooper! I remember that my grandfather used to tell me that on two occasions the people of Tennessee elected a fatherless man to be their governor, and his name was Ben Hooper!"

> ## "YOU ARE A CHILD OF GOD.
> ## DON'T EVER FORGET IT,
> ## ACT LIKE IT,
> ## AND CLAIM YOUR INHERITANCE."

TALKING BACK

1. What would you do to change your appearance to be more acceptable to others? What abilities do you wish that you had that you do not have? Why do you feel inferior, if you feel that you are?

2. How do we know that God's love for us is unconditional, that He loves us just the way we are?

3. Why is it important for an individual to learn to like himself?

4. Why should we avoid playing the comparison game?

5. In your own words, describe what it means that we are "God's workmanship", and that He is working to "conform us to the likeness of his Son."

EXERCISING YOUR FAITH

1. Reflect for a moment. List ten words that describe who you are:

Now list ten words that describe who you want to be:

Pray that you will be "God's workmanship" to accomplish your second list.

2. Complete this sentence: "I feel good about myself because ..." Begin and end each day this week with this sentence.

SUICIDE

Dick Marcear, Minister of the Central Church of Christ in Amarillo, Texas, wrote this bulletin article some time ago:

"Her name was Mary Bowen. She first came to church several years ago. She had walked over four miles by herself to get here. She was a teenager — bright, energetic, full of love and very beautiful. She had heard a spot I had done on the radio about the church being a place of love, warmth and friendship. After several weeks of study, she obeyed the Gospel.

"For the next three years, she was faithful, involved and growing in her Christian life. Then one evening, I got a call — Mary was dead. She had shot herself.

"I rushed to her home. Her parents were divorced, and she lived with her dad. I went into the room where she shot herself. Blood, blood and more blood.

"On her walls were handouts she had received in our Bible school. Also listed were her goals for the year. They read: 1. Put God first in my life; 2. Everyday let the beauty of Jesus be seen in my life; 3. ... 4. ...

"She was a beautiful, charming, articulate young lady. Why? This was Tuesday evening. Sunday she had been in Bible school, church, and had stayed late visiting with her friends. She was a high school senior and planned to attend Abilene Christian University in the fall. Her whole life was in front of her.

"The only thing anyone knew that had happened to her was that she and her boyfriend had broken up. Was she depressed? Probably so, though no one had picked it up."

WHY SUICIDE?

Suicide is the 10th leading cause of death in America, but it is second only to traffic accidents as the leading cause of death among teenagers. Approximately 8,000 confirmed suicides of teenagers are reported each year, and only God knows how many more are unconfirmed because they appear to be accidents or were intentionally covered up to protect families from embarrassment.

Why is there such an increase in teen suicide? There may be many reasons, but the primary causes seem to be:

Family Background — The teen years can be full of emotional swings, self-doubt and searches for identity. Teens dealing with such emotional difficulties need to be able to turn to their families for support and guidance. But, unfortunately, for many teens home is a source of problems, not solutions.

Media — Music, movies, video, television, magazines and books can wittingly or unwittingly encourage suicidal tendencies. Some movies or books encourage a romantic notion of "watching others cry at my funeral." The obvious flaw in this reasoning is that the person won't be around to see the reactions. De-romanticizing and de-glamorizing suicide can literally be a life saver.

Pressure of Competition — Academic, athletic and social pressures seem to be increasing with each generation. Many children have been forced to leave childhood or even adolescence prematurely and make too many adult decisions before they are prepared to do so. This pressure of competition and premature growing up can influence teens negatively.

Biological and/or Chemical Problems — Depression, a central element behind many suicides, can be caused by a deficiency in a brain chemical called serotonin. If the depression is not biologically related, it may stem from rejection or a lack of love and support, whether real or perceived. Such biological or chemical imbalances can lead to suicidal thoughts and perhaps even the act.

Drugs and Alcohol — The stresses of everyday life for a teen are intensified by substance abuse. Some suicide is, in fact, the way a drug- or alcohol-addicted teen attempts to escape from his or her dependency.

These are just a few of the more common reasons for suicide attempts. Perhaps the greatest tragedy of teenage suicide is that many of these deaths are preventable. Danger signals and warning signs almost always precede the actual attempt, and more suicides could be prevented if people were better able to detect the warnings. However, many professionals in the health field often miss suicidal clues, so do not feel guilty if you missed a danger signal in a loved one or friend.

WARNING SIGNS

If you fear that someone is becoming suicidal, insist that others pay attention. The worst you can do is to be wrong and feel responsible for stirring up a suicide scare where none exists. But you do far better to err in the direction of over-caution than to ignore warning signs.

Telling another person about a friend's suicidal plans or threats may mean making a painful decision to break a confidence. Your first responsibility in any potentially suicidal situation is to preserve life, not friendship. After all, there will be no friendship without life. The secret you were asked to keep was not an ordinary one. In fact, it may have been a disguised message or a plea for help. Taking the information given you as being serious and acting upon it is usually best.

What are some of the warning signs that might help you identify a potentially suicidal friend? The most common signs are abrupt changes in behavior:

- A withdrawal from friends, family or activities they once enjoyed. Extreme isolation is often where suicidal thoughts are fed.
- A preoccupation with death and dying.
- A sudden decline in the quality of a student's school work, or truancy from school.
- The making of "final arrangements," such as giving away prized possessions.
- A marked change in eating or sleeping habits or an unexplained loss of energy over a long period of time.

Of course, verbal warning signs are the easiest to recognize. Unfortunately, they are often shrugged off as a bid for attention. One of the biggest myths about suicide is that a person who talks about it will not really attempt it. Some studies indicate that eight out of 10 persons who repeat verbal suicide threats eventually attempt it.

Verbal warning signals may be direct ("What would you think if I killed myself?") or indirect ("Everyone would be better off if I weren't around"). In any event, verbal threats must be taken seriously. Remember, it is far better to over-react than to under-react where suicide threats are concerned.

Warning signals concerning circumstances in life over which a young person has little or no control may also be present. Some examples might be:

- Divorce of parents
- Life-threatening illness or death of a parent.
- Leaving friends and family behind in a family move.
- The breakup of a romance.
- The suicide of a friend or relative.
- The failure to achieve some important goal.

Suicidal warning signals can be difficult to correctly identify because so many of them may also be attributed to typical stressful teenage behavior. However, because of their potential for harm, be aware of these warning signs, particularly if a combination of several of them are present at the same time.

WHAT TO DO

Christians who believe in the dignity of human life and the eternal nature of the soul have a responsibility to help potentially suicidal people. What can you do to help a troubled friend, family member or fellow Christian?

1. Be a real friend. Teens need to know that they can call someone anytime. If one has a relationship with the Lord and with another available, caring friend, he or she is less likely to attempt suicide.

2. Ask questions of a friend if you suspect he or she is suicidal. Your asking will not plant the idea in his or her mind, but it will let him or her know that you realize something is wrong, that you care, and that you will help.

3. Encourage them to keep active and busy in some meaningful task. Suicidal people often become more and more withdrawn and inactive. Encouraging them to maintain a balanced schedule of work, school, recreation and social activities can help them gain a new perspective.

4. Don't attempt to shock or challenge them with statements like, "Go ahead and do it." Don't try to analyze their motives, either. Leave that work to mental health professionals.

5. Try to stay close to them until help is available or until the risk has passed. The feeling of loneliness overwhelms all of us at times. Show you care by your willingness to "be there for them."

6. Pray. Pray for them and with them. Call upon God to help. Encourage them in prayer to rely on such passages as:

> **1 Peter 5:7** — "Cast all your anxiety on him because he cares for you."
> **Hebrews 13:5** — "God has said, 'Never will I leave you; never will I forsake you.'"

Romans 8:28 — "And we know that in all things God works for the good of those who love him, who have been called according to his purpose."

Isaiah 41:10 — "So do not fear, for I am with you; do not be dismayed, for I am your God. I will strengthen you and help you; I will uphold you with my righteous right hand."

Romans 15:13 — "May the God of hope fill you with all joy and peace as you trust in him, so that you may overflow with hope by the power of the Holy Spirit."

7. Finally, and perhaps most importantly, help the person to seek qualified, professional help. Several sources of such help are available:

- **Crisis or suicide prevention centers** — They provide emergency advice and referrals.
- **Mental health centers** — These are usually operated by a hospital, community organization or independent agency.
- **Mental health professionals** — These might include physicians, psychiatrists, psychologists, social workers or school counselors.
- **Ministers and church staff** — They usually can provide some help, depending upon their degree of training and/or experience.

Every day 10 more young people in America take their own lives, and hundreds more attempt to do so. If just one extra life can be saved because a friend learned how to help, then progress will have been made.

Christian teens in particular are in a unique position to counter this enemy of life called suicide. We believe that the Lord Jesus Christ came so that we may "have life, and have it to the full" (John 10:10). Let's share that message of life with everyone, particularly those who are troubled.

TALKING BACK

1. Look over the list of primary causes of teen suicide given in the lesson. Which of these causes do you think is most significant? Are there other causes you can identify?

2. Should you tell another person about a friend's suicidal threats? Explain your answer.

3. What are some of the warning signs that might help you identify a potentially suicidal friend?

4. Discuss the options available for you and your friends in getting qualified, professional help when faced with severe mental or emotional troubles.

5. What can you do personally to help a troubled friend, family member or fellow Christian?

EXERCISING YOUR FAITH

1. Pretend for a moment that you have a friend named Mary who is considering suicide. You want to help her and decide to write her a letter. Write a letter to her in an attempt to help.

2. Call a crises or suicide prevention center and volunteer to help. Or, go to your school guidance counselor and volunteer to help.

FRIENDS

A FRIEND IS ONE WHO KNOWS ALL ABOUT YOU AND LOVES YOU JUST THE SAME.

These were the words on a plaque given to my wife by some very good friends as we were moving out of their community to another town. From time to time we look plaque and remember the friends who gave it to us nearly a decade ago.

We all need friends. We are just fooling ourselves if we think otherwise. Friends are very important to us because they fulfill a multitude of needs in our lives. They provide emotional stability, support, love, acceptance and strength.

There are different levels of friendship. Three easily identifiable levels would include: casual friends, close friends and best friends.

Casual friends are those with whom we occasionally interact in the normal course of living. They may include classmates at school, teammates in sports, neighbors, church friends and many others. These friendships may last for a short time, a longer period of time, or even a lifetime, depending upon various circumstances.

Close friends usually come from the same circle of friends as casual friends, but the relationships deepen over a period of time. These friends may remain close to us for several years,

79

even when circumstances (such as one of them moving) keep them physically apart from us.

Best friends are those to whom we pour out our feelings. They meet our needs, and we meet their needs. These friendships require much time, effort, energy and personal involvement, but they are a source of much joy and strength in our life.

WHAT IS A FRIEND?

Pause for a moment to answer this question: What is a friend? Define "friendship." That is a difficult assignment, isn't it? It is somewhat like trying to define "beauty" — it is in the eye of the beholder. Although it may be challenging to answer, "What is a friend?" let us give it a good try:

A friend is someone who loves you. Proverbs 17:17 reads, "A friend loves at all times, and a brother is born for adversity." True friends love during good times and bad times. "Fair-weather" friends who only stand by us when times are good are not of much value. A true friend "loves at all times" and is "born for adversity."

A friendship is a relationship that we choose. We do not choose our mothers, our fathers, our brothers or sisters, our teachers or many other people who are important in our lives. But we do choose our friends, and that is an honor and trust that we give to one another.

A friend is someone to have fun with, someone who makes you happy. Proverbs 27:9 reads, "Perfume and incense bring joy to the heart, and the pleasantness of one's friend springs from his earnest counsel." We get a special feeling from our friends that makes us want to be with them. Friends laugh, joke, enjoy and have fun together.

A friend is someone who encourages you. We all need to be encouraged and to encourage others. Friendships that consistently drag you down and make you feel depressed cannot survive. We can encourage our friends in many ways — by being there when they need us; through conversation, a letter or a gift; or through prayer. Without this encouragement from friends, life can be discouraging.

A friend considers the need of a friend to be his need as well. When a friend is in need, you should be in need. When a friend suffers, you should suffer. When a friend rejoices, you should rejoice (Romans 12:15). When a need is seen in the life of a friend, a true friend will begin seeking ways of filling this need.

A friend may feel like a member of your family. Friendship ties can become closer than some family ties. This was certainly true of the beautiful friendship between David and King Saul's son, Jonathan (1 Samuel 18-20; 2 Samuel 1:17-27). The Bible speaks of "a friend who sticks closer than a brother" (Proverbs 18:24). Of course, close Christian friends are, in a sense, part of our family since we belong to the "family of God."

A friend brings out the best in you. The great automaker Henry Ford once said, "My best friend is the one who brings out the best in me." Some people bring out the worst in us through destructive criticism, petty gossip or complaining, immaturity or by encouraging us to do wrong. A true friend wants what is best for us and, even when confronting us about a problem, will seek to do so through constructive criticism or positive change. How we all need friends who will seek to bring out the best in us!

Certainly, this is not a complete definition of a friend, but it is a good start. What additional qualities would you mention as being important to friendship?

One other important quality is that a true friend should be interested in your spiritual needs as well as your physical and emotional needs. The truth is, friends drive you to or from God. Proverbs 13:20 reads, "He who walks with the wise grows wise, but a companion of fools suffers harm." And Paul wrote, "Do not be misled: 'Bad company corrupts good character'" (1 Corinthians 15:33). We need friends who pray for us and take some interest in our spiritual lives. And, in being a friend, we need to encourage others to a closer walk with God.

WHAT TO DO

Sometimes teens experience difficulty in making friends. This is particularly true when one moves to a new town, changes schools, changes churches or old friends move away from us. How well I remember the apprehension I felt as a high school sophomore when I moved to a completely new school where I knew no one!

If a new friendship is going to develop, someone must take the initiative to make the first move. Many obstacles must be overcome in making new friends (fear of rejection, lack of time, being introverted or shy), but the rewards are worth the effort. Cultivating such friendships can become one of life's greatest blessings — so go for it!

But wait a minute. How do you go about initiating new friendships? Let's consider a few practical suggestions for launching out and making new friends:

1. Be more concerned with being a friend than having a friend. Too many people are only concerned with having friends, those who will meet their needs. Not as many are interested in being a friend, concentrating on meeting the needs of another. If you will spend more time concentrating on *being* a friend rather than just *having* friends, you will never lack for true friends.

2. Be willing to try taking the first step toward friendship. Someone must take the first step, and it might as well be you. What can you do to take that first step? Try a smile, a kind note, a phone call, or an invitation to your home.

3. Don't be too concerned about rejection. Realize that everyone you reach out to will not be open to new friendships, and it may not have anything at all to do with you personally. The other person may simply have all the relationships he can handle at that time, or he may have personal problems that would prevent the forming of a new friendship at the time. If rejected by one person, simply try again with someone else.

4. Actively work on making yourself more attractive to others. Smile more. Lighten up. Really listen to others. Be positive. Offer compliments freely. Build another person up. Laugh. Enjoy the company of others.

We need to initiate new friendships for our own benefit, for the benefit of others, and for the enjoyment of life. God really knew He was planning for our needs when He created friendship.

THE BEST OF FRIENDS

How can one be a good friend? As we consider that question, let's take a look at perhaps the best story of friendship in the Bible — the friendship between Jonathan and David.

Jonathan was the son of King Saul. He witnessed the great victory that God had given David over Goliath and was so impressed that he wanted David for a friend. It seems that in choosing a friend, Jonathan was looking for: 1. someone who trusted God in crisis; 2. someone with courage to stand for his convictions; and 3. someone who could help him get closer to God.

What kind of friend was Jonathan to David? Jonathan loved David as much as he loved himself, and he began giving to David to express his love and friendship (1 Samuel 18:3-4). The sacrifices that Jonathan made for David were a testimony to their deep friendship. What sacrifices did he make?

Keep in mind that Jonathan was the son of the king. By natural progression, he would be the heir to the throne of Israel. But because Jonathan truly loved David and recognized that David was God's choice for the next king, he was willing to put aside his own desires and support David.

Jonathan had to take a stand against his own father while helping David (1 Samuel 19-20), which was certainly a test of his loyalty in friendship. Jonathan even put his own life on the line by standing up for David, after learning of his father's wicked plot to attempt David's murder.

Second Samuel 1:17-27 records David's words of sorrow when he learned of Jonathan's death. They are a moving tribute to the friendship that existed between these two godly men: "I grieve for you, Jonathan my brother, you were very dear to me. Your love for me was wonderful, more wonderful than that of women" (v. 26).

What lessons on friendship can we learn from the story of Jonathan and David?

Always recognize the value in true friendship, and treasure it. Friendship is a sacred trust. When others say, "You are my friend," they are entrusting you with something very important to them. The word "friend," as translated from the New Testament, literally means "one dearly beloved" or "one held precious and dear." Never be guilty of taking good friends for granted. Treasure them.

Jonathan's motives were right in doing good for David's benefit. We should not do something for others to: 1. make them like us; 2. make them feel an obligation to us; or 3. bring glory or praise to ourselves. Kind deeds naturally flow from a warm, loving friendship.

Friendship may involve sacrifice. Jonathan's friendship with David cost him the good will of his father, and perhaps even the throne of Israel. And, of course, Jesus' friendship with us cost Him His life: "Greater love has no one than this, that he lay down his life for his friends" (John 15:13). True friendship gives and gives, knowing no bounds of sacrifice.

The benefits of true friendship are lasting, perhaps even beyond death. In 2 Samuel 9 we see that David did a favor for Jonathan's son, Mephibosheth, in honor of Jonathan well after his death. Mephibosheth was crippled, but David brought him to the palace to live as one of his own sons. Some have criticized David for waiting too late to express such friendship to Jonathan. Whether he did or not, it is true that many people today wait too long to express love for their friends. We should act upon our "good intentions" and do now what we plan to do later for our friends. Let's show our appreciation and love now while we can!

Jonathan loved David as much as he loved himself (1 Samuel 18:3). Close friendships encourage this kind of love. Remember that Jesus said to "'Love the Lord your God with all your heart and with all your soul and with all your mind.' This is the first and greatest commandment. And the second is like it: 'Love your neighbor as yourself'" (Matthew 22:37-39). God can give a love for a friend that is comparable to a love for self. How precious is such a friendship!

As musician Michael W. Smith and his wife, Debbie, wrote in the well known song "Friends":

> And friends are friends forever
> If the Lord's the Lord of them.

Good Christian friends can be friends forever! It is truly a wonderful blessing of God to be a friend and to have a friend!

TALKING BACK

1. Define these terms: casual friends; close friends; best friends.

2. A friendship is a relationship we choose. Why is that significant and special?

3. Discuss some ways we can encourage our friends. What does a friend do that makes you feel encouraged or inspired?

4. Do you agree that friends drive you to or from God? Explain your answer.

5. What does it mean in the lesson when it says we should be more concerned with being a friend than having a friend?

EXERCISING YOUR FAITH

1. Describe in words or short phrases what you want in a friend. List at least 6-8 words or phrases.

   Go back over your list and assess what kind of friend you are to others.

2. This week write letter of support, appreciation, encouragement, etc., to at least two or three of your friends.

PAIN

A friend of mine named Rick had been dating a girl named Cindy for three years. Having dated all through high school, they were best friends and constant companions, and now, during their early college years, they were unofficially engaged. They had already named their future children, planned their future careers, and shaped many of their jointly held values and dreams.

Then, out of the blue, Cindy broke off their relationship and announced to Rick that she didn't want to date him anymore. For Rick, it was the closest one could get to divorce without marriage. "Hurt" does not fully describe the pain of his emotional state. "Crushed" perhaps comes a little closer.

Hurt feelings. We all have them at some time or another. Painful memories. What we did or what others did to us. Angers. Heartaches. Tears. Emotional suffering. Injustices. Violations of our spirit. Memories of hurt so potent that we think they can never be forgotten or escaped.

What do you do when you don't know what to do about that kind of hurt, that kind of pain? We all need answers, solutions to this vital question. Search with me for answers to the problem of deep, emotional pain.

WHAT <u>NOT</u> TO DO

First of all, we should discuss what *not* to do with the hurts you experience.

Don't ignore or suppress your pain. My friend Rick chose initially to play the "macho man" and suppress his hurt. He acted like he was not hurting very much, but most of his friends suspected he was just covering up. Rick immersed himself in a frenzy of work and activity. He planned activity for virtually every minute of his waking hours to avoid thinking about the breakdown of his relationship with Cindy. Sometime later, he broke down physically, mentally and emotionally because he had attempted to bury the hurt rather than deal with it.

Learn to be honest about your pain and talk about it with friends. Sometimes we may need the help of a minister, or Christian counselor, or other mental health professional to talk out such feelings. Ignoring or suppressing them not only doesn't work, but it creates more problems later on.

Second, don't retreat into a shell. When we have been hurt, we naturally tend to want to withdraw so that we will not be hurt again. We think, "I've been betrayed and let down, and I will not allow it to happen again." As a result, we may pull back from people.

Withdrawal is most tempting when we have been hurt in a relationship. Rick thought he could never love again. He kept saying, "How could Cindy do this to me? How can I ever love and trust anyone again?" The truth is, loving again helps bring about healing for the hurt. Retreating into a shell is not the answer for dealing with emotional pain.

Third, don't dwell on the past. Once you have dealt with your hurts, refuse to live in yesterday. Satan is the one who likes for us to wallow around in the garbage of yesterday. As long as Satan can keep us dwelling on yesterday, he knows he is defeating us today!

Paul's words are particularly relevant at this point. Here was a man who had persecuted Christians and had been a leader in opposing the cause of Christ before becoming a Christian himself. Yet, he wrote concerning his past: "But one thing I do: Forgetting what is behind and straining toward what is ahead, I press on toward the goal to win the prize for which God has called me heavenward in Christ Jesus" (Philippians 3:13-14). Like Paul, sometimes we must "forget what is behind" in order to heal the hurts of our past and move successfully into the future!

Fourth, don't give up the good things of life just because you have been hurt. Rick was tempted to give up completely on relationships and not date again. His attitude was, "Never will I be hurt like this again. I will not fall in love ever again and run the risk of being hurt." But he didn't realize that such an attitude was causing him to continue hurting and hurting all the more.

We may lose a love relationship — but that doesn't mean all love relationships are bad. We may be betrayed by a friend — but that doesn't mean all friends are bad. We may experience rejection from a parent — but that doesn't mean all parents or guardians are bad.

Jesus is our best example here. He had hurts, being "a man of sorrows, and familiar with suffering" (Isaiah 53:3). Early in His ministry, Jesus returned to his hometown of Nazareth. Everyone wants to be loved and accepted in his hometown and, undoubtedly, Jesus was no exception. The curious townspeople turned out to hear his message, but they didn't like what he had to say. In fact, Luke 4:28-29 records, "All the people in the synagogue were furious when they heard this. They got up, drove him out of the town, and took him to the brow of the hill on which the town was built, in order to throw him down the cliff."

Although He escaped, it must have hurt Jesus a great deal to have been rejected by His hometown folks — those He had known, loved and grown up with. Yet, He didn't give up preaching, teaching and serving just because Nazareth rejected Him. Follow Jesus' example, and don't give up on the good things of life just because you may have experienced emotional hurt.

WHAT TO DO

By now, you are probably thinking to yourself, "That's just great! You've told me a lot of things that I shouldn't do when I've been hurt. How about some things I can do that will help heal the hurt?" OK, let's give it a try:

1. Admit that you are hurting whenever you feel emotional pain. By the way, I'm not talking about the little hurts we may experience every day, the things that do not deserve much attention in the first place. However, we must deal with the major hurts in our lives or they will haunt us later in other ways.

I have a friend who felt emotionally abused by his parents during his childhood. He is now estranged from them and hasn't seen them in years. The trauma of his experience has caused him to have enormous problems in making and maintaining relationships with others. But instead of reconciling with his parents and beginning a process of forgiveness and healing, he internalizes it, and the hurt continues to linger. He refuses to admit that he has been greatly hurt, although his friends can clearly see the hurt in him.

The first step toward solving any problem is to admit there is a problem. And the sooner one admits to his hurt and applies healing to it, the better off he will be.

2. Accept the fact that you will experience some hurts in life. Getting all bent out of shape over all the hurts another person may cause you is senseless. Expect occasional hurts in life, and pre-determine to just go on anyway. Remember the "Serenity Prayer" from the chapter on dealing with your parents (Chapter 6):

> God grant me the serenity to accept the things I cannot change, the courage to change the things I can, and the wisdom to know the difference.

Try praying it when you feel hurt — and believe it — understand that:

- **You cannot change another person.** Neither can you change the past or the hurts you may have experienced in the past. You might as well accept that truth.

- **You do need God's courage to change what you can control.** You can change how you respond to people who have hurt you. You can choose to "love your enemies and pray for those who persecute you" (Matthew 5:44). You can change how you react to the hurts that come your way. You can allow God to help you in your hurts, rather than being upset that He doesn't insulate you from your hurts.

- **You can pray for the wisdom to know the difference between little everyday hurts that are not worthy of our attention, and the kind of emotional pain that will not go away until it is resolved.** You can pray for God's wisdom to help you know what to do when you don't know what to do.

3. Allow the healing power of forgiveness to help you with your hurts. Don't nurture the pain. Satan loves to see you holding onto your hurts and pains. Refuse to give him the pleasure of having a foothold in your life (Ephesians 4:26-27).

Nothing is more healing than when one offers forgiveness and accepts forgiveness. It is not always easy to forgive, but in the long run, it is more difficult not to forgive. When we fail to extend forgiveness to those who have hurt us, we reject the way of Christ and set ourselves up for more pain.

Are you experiencing hurt? If so, why? Have your parents caused you emotional pain? Have your brothers or sisters failed you? Has a boyfriend or girlfriend rejected you? Has a friend betrayed you? Have classmates teased you, made fun of you or put you down? Has someone else hurt you?

If so, here is a major part of the solution. FORGIVE! Only by offering and accepting forgiveness can we begin to put the past pain behind us and experience healing for our hurt.

4. Act in faith to decrease the hurt in your life. There are several actions we can take to reduce emotional pain:

- **Refuse to live in the past.** Allowing yourself to be miserable in the present because of some pain in the past is a waste of time and energy. The past cannot be recalled or relived — or changed. What has happened has happened. Too much living in the past will cause failure in the present. We must dismiss such thoughts of living in the past as a Satanic effort to defeat us.

- **Do your best to live successfully today.** Focus on today's blessings, hopes and opportunities. Counteract the pain of yesterday by counting the blessings of today. Making something positive out of something that has been negative is a major step in conquering hurt. Make King David's prayer your prayer: "This is the day the Lord has made; let us rejoice and be glad in it" (Psalm 118:24).

- **Use your past hurt as a teacher.** When hurt comes, remember that God is in control (Romans 8:28). He often permits pain to come into our lives to teach us something. In the midst of your pain, God could be trying to teach you a lesson about Himself or about His will for your life. Ask yourself, "Is there some important lesson or principle God may be trying to teach me through this hurt? Is there some way this can "work out for my good" (Romans 8:28). Although we may not see it at the time, some good usually results from the bad things that may happen to us. Look for the lessons God may want you to learn.

- **Lean on the Lord, and trust Him to heal your hurt.** Tell the Lord about your feelings. Describe to Him the depth of your pain. He specializes in "healing the broken-hearted"(Luke 4:18 KJV). He said, "Come to me, all you who are weary and burdened, and I will give you rest" (Matthew 11:28). We have the only faith in the world that can make this kind of promise and back it up — lean on Him!

Perhaps you are wondering how my friend Rick turned out. Did he overcome his hurt? Did he ever learn to love and trust again? I am happy to tell you that he most definitely did. He is now married to a beautiful woman who he loves far more than he ever loved Cindy. They have two precious children. He has a good job that he enjoys very much. The hurt and pain have been replaced by love, trust and joy.

By the way, his real name is not Rick. I gave him that name as a pseudonym to cover up his identity. His real name is Randy — as in me.

I've personally experienced what I am writing about in this chapter. These biblical suggestions helped me overcome my hurt and go on to something better — and they can help you, too.

TALKING BACK

1. How do you react or respond when your feelings are hurt?

2. What are some unhealthy responses to hurt feelings? And why are they unhealthy?

3. What are some healthy responses to hurt feelings? And why are they healthy and productive?

4. Why is Jesus best able to help us deal with hurt feelings? What do you think would be Jesus' message to us concerning the hurt we may feel?

5. How can we learn to use hurts from our past as a teacher for our future?

EXERCISING YOUR FAITH

1. Memorize the "Serenity Prayer" given in the lesson. Repeat it every time you experience hurt feelings.

2. Seek out someone else who is presently experiencing emotional pain. Offer them the help and support you would want if you were in their situation.

FAILURE

t was a beautiful and bright Sunday afternoon in Ana-
heim, Calif. Game 5 of the 1986 American League
Championship Series was being played between the
Boston Red Sox and the California Angels. The Angels were leading the best-of-seven series three games to one,
and were leading this game by one run as they moved to the
top the ninth inning. They were one inning away from ad-
vancing to the first World Series in their team's history.

Trying to ensure their win, the Angels brought in their ace
relief pitcher, Donnie Moore, who had led them in saved games
for two seasons. As the ninth inning progressed, the Red Sox
had a runner on first with two men out and outfielder Dave
Henderson at the plate. Moore quickly got two strikes on Henderson. The Angels were one strike away from their long-await-
ed first World Series!

Dave Henderson hit Donnie Moore's next pitch over the left
field fence for a two-run home run to win the game for Boston.
Furthermore, Boston won the next two games to win the Championship Series four games to three, depriving the Angels of going to the World Series.

Donnie Moore was devastated. His despondency grew into a
chronic depression that was complicated by problems at home
and a sore pitching arm that forced him into an early retire-
ment. Then, tragically, on July 19, 1989, Moore committed sui-

cide after shooting his wife in front of their children.

Everyone who knew Donnie Moore well — his wife, children, agent, fellow ball players and friends — said it was the failure of his pitching in Game 5 of the 1986 Series that caused his deep depression and eventual attempted murder and suicide. One of his friends said, "He never got over that game. It haunted him constantly. He tried so hard to be accepted by others. It's very sad because it's only a game."

WE ALL FAIL

One common denominator unites every person in the world — failure. We may come from different families, backgrounds and cultures, and we may have different skills, interests and abilities, but every one of us has at least one thing in common — we have tasted the agony of failure.

Failure can be a jarring experience, but we should always remember that failure doesn't have to be final. In fact, failure can be the first step on the road to success. Consider some illustrations of this vital truth:

- Babe Ruth struck out 1,330 times during his baseball career, but he also hit 714 home runs, the second most in the history of baseball.

- Abraham Lincoln failed in seven different elections before finally being elected president of the United States, and he has been voted our greatest president ever in several polls.

- Robert Louis Stevenson's first book was so heartlessly condemned by the critics that he contemplated suicide, but he went on to become one of the world's greatest authors.

- Thomas Edison was working on finding a substitute for lead in the manufacture of storage batteries. Edison informed a visitor that he had made 1,000 experiments, but none of them had worked. His friend asked, "Aren't you discouraged by all this waste of effort?" Edison replied,

"There is nothing wasted. I have found 1,000 things that will not work, but I am closer to something that will work." Of course, he was successful later with this invention and many others.

Learning that failure doesn't have to be final is not limited to contemporary illustrations. God's Word is filled with examples of people who learned that failure may actually be a springboard to victory:

- *David* failed in his sin of adultery and murder, but he was recreated by God (Psalm 51:10) and became the only man the Bible ever called "a man after God's own heart" (1 Samuel 13:14 KJV).

- *John Mark* failed on his first missionary journey (Acts 15:37-38), but he later became very useful in ministry (2 Timothy 4 :11).

- *Peter* denied Jesus in the shadow of the cross, cursing and swearing that he did not even know Him. A short time later Peter preached the great sermon on the Day of Pentecost when the church began, and then became a great apostle and leader in the early church.

GOOD FAILURE?

Failure doesn't have to be final; in fact, failure can be very good for you. When is failure good for you?

Failure is good when it teaches humility. Nothing teaches humility like a little failure. If we were successful in every single undertaking, we would be filled with pride and be very difficult to be around. Most of us learn much more from our defeats than from our victories. In defeat we tend to evaluate, whereas in victory we tend to celebrate. So defeats or failures can be of great value to us if we learn from them and use them to help us mature.

Failure is good when it teaches us to be dependent on God, not just ourselves. A little failure can knock a lot of overconfident nonsense out of us by revealing our weaknesses and our need for God.

Failure is good when it teaches us compassion and sympathy for others. Our own failures can make us more understanding and accepting, and less judgmental and condemning of other people. Galatians 6:1-2 teaches that we are to have love for those who have fallen into sin. The person who has undergone the experience of falling is far less likely to throw stones at those who are now falling — and he is much more likely to "carry the burdens" of others.

Failure can be good for us when it emphasizes the greatness of God's grace. The person who can best understand the depths of God's amazing grace is the one who has failed and been forgiven. Peter is a good example of this great truth. I can just imagine what Peter must have said to his audiences: "Look at me. I denied the Lord. I turned my back on Him at his trial and at the cross when He needed me the most. And still He loved me and forgave me. And what Jesus did for me, He can and will do for you."

All of us have the choice of using our failures as an ingredient for more failure — or of taking those same failures, learning from them and going forward, making them an ingredient for success.

MORE THAN CONQUERORS

God made us to succeed, not fail. The Bible has much to say about our being successful:

> "Blessed is the man who does not walk in the counsel of the wicked or stand in the way of sinners or sit in the seat of mockers. But his delight is in the law of the Lord, and on his law he meditates day and night. He is like a tree planted by streams of water, which yields its fruit in season and whose leaf does not wither. Whatever he does prospers" (Psalm 1:1-3).

> "But thanks be to God! He gives us the victory through our Lord Jesus" (1 Corinthians 15:57).

> "I can do everything through him who gives me strength" (Philippians 4:13).

"We are more than conquerors through him who loved us" (Romans 8:37).

God didn't say, "You are more than flops" or "You are more than failures," but "You are more than conquerors!" Now, in the making of us to be "more than conquerors," God may use, among other things, failure. Most of us fail before we succeed. We don't start everything as a rousing success story. Satan often uses temporary failures to discourage Christians, particularly teens and new Christians who may fail a few times and just give up, thinking it's all over. That, my friends, is one of Satan's biggest lies! God's Word says that you can be a conqueror, a victor.

WHAT TO DO

How can we conquer our failures? What can we do when we don't know what to do about failure? Here are a few simple suggestions:

1. Realize that "to err is human." God does not expect perfection from us. He made us and is fully aware of our capacity for failure: "For he knows how we are formed, he remembers that we are dust" (Psalm 103:14). It may help to remember that "all have sinned and fall short of the glory of God" (Romans 3:23).

2. Don't be too hard on yourself when you have failed in some way. Give yourself some breathing room. Give yourself permission to bat less than 1.000 in the game of life. Loosen up a bit and relax, giving yourself permission to be human.

3. Don't excuse or rationalize your failures, but rather work to correct them. While it is true that we shouldn't be too hard on ourselves, neither should we be too easy on ourselves, simply excusing or rationalizing away our faults or failure. God has said for us to "confess your sins [faults, failures] to each other and pray for each other so that you may be healed" (James 5:16).

4. Use your failures as a door to success. Don't waste your failures by ignoring them or wallowing in self-pity. Instead, learn from your mistakes and follow the instructions of the apostle Paul: "Whatever you do, work at it with all your heart, as working for the Lord, not for men, since you know that you will receive an inheritance from the Lord as a reward. It is the Lord Christ you are serving" (Colossians 3:23-24).

An unknown poet wrote:

> What is failure? It is only a spur,
> To the one who received it right;
> It makes the spirit within him stir,
> To go in once more and fight.
> If you've never failed,
> It's an easy guess;
> That you've also never won,
> Any high success.

Fear of failure paralyzes many people from even trying to successfully do the will of God. Someone has said, "Better to have tried something great and failed than to have tried nothing at all and succeeded." How true! Pray that God will help you to use your failures as a springboard to success.

5. Whatever you do, don't quit because of failure. Don't complain or become depressed, thinking you are a nobody who might as well give up. It is no disgrace to fail; in fact, it is quite common. It is a disgrace, however, to just completely give up and quit. Hang in there, remembering the words of Paul: "I have fought the good fight, I have finished the race, I have kept the faith. Now there is in store for me the crown of righteousness, which the Lord, the righteous Judge, will award to me on that day — and not only to me, but also to all who have longed for his appearing" (2 Timothy 4:7-8).

Jim Ryun is one of the greatest track stars in the history of American sports. In 1964 at the age of 17, he became the first high school student to run the mile in less than four minutes. During his career he established several world records, but his real goal was to win the gold medal for the mile run in the Olympic Games.

Day after day, week after week, year after year, Ryun trained for the 1972 Olympic Games in Munich, West Germany. His training was intensive and brutal, running several miles every day and working with weights, while maintaining a proper diet. The gold medal was his dream, his goal.

Finally, after years of preparation, the race for the gold began. Early in the race, Ryun's foot became entangled with the foot of another runner, and the two of them fell to the track.

What a misfortune! All those years of training and dreaming seemed to be down the drain because of an unfortunate accident!

But what happened next has inspired people for years. The other runner got up, cleaned himself off, and walked off the track, realizing that the other runners were so far ahead that he could only finish last or next to last.

Jim Ryun got up and, after quickly checking himself for injury, began to run as fast as he could. He knew that he couldn't finish anywhere but last — but he could finish! He had experienced failure in his goal of winning the gold medal, but was Jim Ryun a failure? No way! In many ways, he was the greatest success story of all the runners (I don't even remember who won the race).

You may not always "win" the fight. You may experience some failure. But you can "finish the race and keep the faith." That is all God expects of you.

TALKING BACK

1. What would you do to change your appearance to be more acceptable to others? What abilities do you wish that you had that you do not have? Why do you feel inferior, if you feel that you are?

2. How do we know that God's love for us is unconditional, that He loves us just the way we are?

3. Why is it important for an individual to learn to like himself?

4. Why should we avoid playing the comparison game?

5. In your own words, describe what it means that we are "God's workmanship", and that He is working to "conform us to the likeness of his Son."

EXERCISING YOUR FAITH

1. Reflect for a moment. List ten words that describe who you are:

   Now list ten words that describe who you want to be:

   Pray that you will be "God's workmanship" to accomplish your second list.

2. Complete this sentence: "I feel good about myself because ..." Begin and end each day this week with this sentence.

DOUBTS

Perhaps some of you are like me. I grew up in a Christian home and attended the services of the church every time the door was opened. I had Christian friends. Beginning with my sophomore year in high school, I attended a Christian school. But I also had moments when I was filled with doubts. I wondered:

- "Is the Bible really true?"
- "Is Jesus really the Son of God?"
- "Where did I come from?"
- "Where am I going?"
- "Is there a God?"

These are disturbing questions that pierce to the soul. If we can answer them confidently, I believe we have the blueprint for success in the Christian life. But as long as we have serious doubts about these questions and others like them, it will be very difficult for us to be truly excited about Christianity.

DEALING WITH DOUBT

Faith, if it is to be effective, must be intensely personal and not merely inherited. In all honesty, during my teen years I believe that my faith was inherited from my parents and Bible teachers. While I am grateful for their model and for that inheritance, I also understand that it was not enough. It may satisfy for a little while, but not when the storms of doubt begin to rage within a maturing mind. So, what do you do about doubt?

First of all, understand that questioning one's beliefs and testing one's faith is healthy, for once we find sufficient evidence, our faith is greatly strengthened and doubt is diminished. If the Christian faith is really true (and it is), then it will stand up to whatever reasonable tests are placed upon it. I like what Batsell Barrett Baxter wrote in his book *I Believe Because*: "It is our conviction that in the long run it is better to face problems, find the evidence, and then know the truth about a matter. To remain in ignorance, even though one may be fully satisfied in one's ignorance, is hardly a defensible position."

Second, realize that some doubting is unavoidable. Christianity is first and foremost a way of faith: "We live by faith, not by sight" (2 Corinthians 5:7). If we lived by sight, we would have all the answers and never have any doubts. Living by faith means that we trust God even though we do not completely understand everything about Him. The Bible defines "faith" as "being sure of what we hope for and certain of what we do not see" (Hebrews 11:1). You must believe something. Having studied Christian evidences in depth, I can say with certainty that my believing in God and His Word is not as difficult as believing what I would have to believe otherwise.

Third, understand that doubts can help us grow. We often think of doubts as being destructive, but they can be constructive tools that God uses to push us into a deeper faith. Which is better: a faith that accepts blindly, or a faith that seeks proof? Christianity is not intellectually bankrupt. It rests on a large number of reasonable evidences. Learn to see your doubts as opportunities for growth rather than obstacles to growth.

Fourth, commit to working through your doubts rather than dodging them. Unless we are willing to confront our doubts, our faith will always be on "sinking sand" rather than built on "Christ, the Solid Rock." Face your doubts, ask your questions, and then work like crazy for good answers. This approach will actually strengthen your faith.

I'VE GOT TO SEE IT TO BELIEVE IT

The Bible contains a true story concerning doubt that serves as a model for our consideration. One of Jesus' 12 original disciples was Thomas, often referred to as "doubting Thomas." Perhaps this dedicated disciple has received a bum rap. He had a questioning mind-set that desired to know the truth, but once he knew, he followed Jesus wholeheartedly.

Thomas gets his nickname primarily from an incident in John 20:19-31 concerning Jesus' resurrection. For some reason, Thomas was not present with the other disciples the first night when Jesus appeared to them after His resurrection. When the other disciples told Thomas they had seen Jesus, he said, "Unless I see the nail marks in his hands and put my finger where the nails were, and put my hand into his side, I will not believe it" (v. 25).

Thomas was doubtful, but he was willing to be convinced. He just wasn't willing to live out his life pretending to believe something he didn't. However, he did attend the disciples' next meeting, where Jesus appeared again — causing Thomas to confess, "My Lord and my God!" (v. 28).

Jesus then taught an important eternal truth, saying to Thomas, "Because you have seen me, you have believed; blessed are those who have not seen and yet have believed" (v. 29) Only a few hundred people saw the risen Christ. Millions of other believers have never seen Him except through the eyes of faith.

Faith is the cornerstone of Christianity and the antidote for doubt. Hebrews 11:6 reads, "And without faith it is impossible to please God, because anyone who comes to him must believe that he exists and that he rewards those who earnestly seek him."

There are at least two excellent reasons for fighting our doubts with faith:

1. ***God wants us to develop and use our faith.*** He
wants us to be able to use our faith to combat athe-
ism, unbelief, ignorance and doubt. Peter admon-
ished us to "always be prepared to give an answer to
everyone who asks you to give the reason for the
hope that you have" (1 Peter 3:15). God expects us
to be prepared to give an explanation for our faith
that goes far beyond, "That's what I've always been
taught."

2. ***We need to confront our doubts and develop our
faith for our own peace of mind.*** Lingering doubts,
whether expressed or unexpressed, can literally tor-
ture the person who is sincere about the really important matters of life.

We will never have all the answers we want. Life is not an in-
tellectual puzzle waiting to be figured out; it is instead an excit-
ing adventure waiting to be lived. Our primary challenge is to
have faith that God is in control. Carl Sandberg told about the
white man who drew a small circle in the sand and attempted to
humble the Indian by saying, "This is what the Indian knows."
Then he drew a larger circle around the smaller one, proclaiming,
"This is what the white man knows." The Indian grabbed the stick
and swept an immense circle around both, exclaiming, "This is
where the white man and Indian know nothing."

There are some things in the spiritual realm where that principle holds true. God's Word even tells us that some things will remain mysteries until God sees fit to reveal them in eternity (1
Corinthians 2:7-16). Therefore, faith is really an inner confidence
in God — a confidence that goes beyond the realm of human
knowledge, understanding or explanation.

WHAT TO DO

How can we cultivate greater faith and diminish doubt?

1. We can learn to be patient with our own occasional doubts and the doubts of others. It is very interesting to note that neither Jesus nor the other disciples criticized Thomas for his honest doubt. They didn't shun him in any way, backstab him, or make him feel unwelcomed at their next meeting. They were willing to be patient and give Thomas the opportunity to work through his doubts. If people do not feel comfortable raising honest questions or expressing honest doubts, their spiritual growth will be stunted. No question is settled to the person who sincerely asks it, and every generation has the right to ask the tough questions.

2. Build on the faith you have, and go from there. Faith is not just for overly emotional people who can't make it through life without a crutch. Faith is a part of every person's life. The question is not, "Do we have faith or not?" but, "In what and to what extent do we have faith?" Everyone must believe or have faith in something. Start with the faith you do have, and use it. Act upon it, and it will grow.

3. Feed your faith. Faith will not work on autopilot. It will not automatically remain strong; it must be fed. How do you feed faith? Here's a start:

- Regular Bible study
- A consistent prayer life
- Active fellowship with other Christians
- Meaningful times of worship
- Service to others

Feed your faith with these biblical "meals," and you will see it increase as your doubts decrease.

4. Don't permit your faith to fluctuate because of moods: "For feelings come and feelings go, And feelings are deceiving. My faith is in the Word of God — Nothing else is worth believing."

In his excellent book *Mere Christianity*, C.S. Lewis defined "faith" as "the art of holding on to things your reason has once accepted, in spite of your changing moods." In the New Testament, the word "faith" or "believe" appears nearly 500 times — yet the word "feel" appears only five times, and even then it is not in the context of telling us how to live and act. Base your feelings upon your faith and not your faith upon your feelings!

5. Seek help from mature Christians who understand doubt. Experienced Christians will not be horrified and shocked by your doubts. They will look upon your questions as an opportunity for increasing your faith. They have walked the path of doubt to faith themselves and can be your guide along that path.

6. Stay in church. During painful times of doubt, it can be very easy to drift away from the church and your faith. But the truth is, it is during those times that you need the fellowship of the church more than ever. Resolving your doubts outside the community of the church is very difficult. Stay in the church while you work on increasing your faith and decreasing your doubts.

7. Finally, don't give up on your faith. You have the choice to hang on to your faith or to give up. There are no spiritual shortcuts to great faith. Give God time to work a quality product in you. Don't give up while He's still working on you. If there is any one message I want to leave with you as I close, it is this:

WHEN YOU DON'T KNOW WHAT TO DO ... DON'T QUIT!

God has promised that He will never quit on you — don't you quit on God or yourself.

TALKING BACK

1. Why is it better to have some doubts than to never have had any doubts?

2. What does it mean that effective faith must be intensely personal and not merely inherited?

3. Read 1 Peter 3:15. What do you think this verse means?

4. Why is it true that everyone must believe or have faith in something?

5. Read the definition of faith given by C.S. Lewis in *Mere Christianity*. What do you think Lewis meant? Why must feelings be governed by faith and not faith governed by feelings?

EXERCISING YOUR FAITH

1. Make a list of at least five good questions about the Christian faith that have caused you to wonder, or even doubt, about faith. Ask a minister, youth minister, elder or your parents to discuss your questions with you.

2. Give serious consideration to these statements:
   • If someone asked me to tell them what a Christian is, I would answer ...
   • If someone asked me if I am a Christian, I would answer ...
   • If some one asked me why I am a Christian, I would answer ...
   • The reason I believe in God, Christ, and the Bible is ...

Don't Quit!

When things go wrong, as they sometimes will,
When the road you are trudging seems all uphill,
When the funds are low and the debts are high,
And you want to smile but you have to sigh,
When care is pressing you down a bit,
Rest, if you must — but don't you quit!

Life is queer with its twists and turns,
As every one of us sometimes learns,
And many a failure turns about
When he might have won had he stuck it out;
Don't give up, though the pace seems slow —
You might succeed with another blow.

Success is failure turned inside out —
The silver tint of the clouds of doubt —
And you can never tell how close you are;
It may be near when it seems afar;
So stick to the fight when you are hardest hit —
It's when things get worse that you mustn't quit!

Edgar A. Guest

OTHER BOOKS BY RANDY SIMMONS:

Real Life Lessons for Teens

Basic Training: A Manual for Teens

Straight Talk for Teens

HORIZONS

Bible Studies for Teens From Gospel Advocate:

Horizons is a popular quarterly curriculum written specifically for today's teens by active youth ministers. They know what young people are looking for and how to present sound, biblical lessons so that teens can understand and apply them.

Each quarter is new and follows the same Bible text as Gospel Advocate's popular adult curriculum. Each lesson contains discussion questions, life applications and activities, all designed to help your teens know and live God's truth.